The Exceptional Child

The Exceptional Child

WALTER B. BARBE

*Professor of Special Education
and Department Head
Kent State University*

1963
The Center for Applied Research in Education, Inc.
Washington, D.C.

Foreword

Dr. Walter Barbe has written *The Exceptional Child* with a keen appreciation of the needs of exceptional children which, as he points out, are different only in degree from those of "normal" or "average" children. Throughout this monograph, a point of view is presented that is being increasingly endorsed by teachers; namely, that education is a process in which the optimum development of each pupil is sought in accord with his unique nature and needs. That this worthy objective is being realized to a far greater degree today than in the past is shown by the recent concern about the gifted pupil, as well as by the attention given to brain-injured pupils and to other types long neglected. However, much remains to be accomplished in providing adequate educational opportunities and stimulation for exceptional children. Dr. Barbe's monograph should aid in the cultivation of a more general interest.

This monograph is recommended, not only to teachers of exceptional children, but also to regular classroom teachers who will gain much from reading this sympathetic discussion of the nature, needs, and problems of exceptional children. Teachers will gain too by consideration of Dr. Barbe's discussion of the ways through which the development of such children may be fostered most effectively. It is a pleasure to recommend this timely, provocative monograph.

PAUL WITTY
Northwestern University

Contents

CHAPTER I

Introduction

Education has been defined as "that process which seeks to promote the maximum development of every boy and girl in terms of his unique nature and needs."[1] If we accept this point of view, we are dedicated not only to the education of the average child but to the fullest development of every child regardless of the degree to which he may be different.

Definition

Public schools are concerned with the education of all children, regardless of the degree to which some of their children may differ from others. It is no longer acceptable as good education to apply the same set of standards to all children on the assumption that in ability, temperament, and physical makeup they are all alike. The standards appropriate to the average child are futile and frustrating to the below-average child. Applying average standards to the above-average is equally frustrating, and wasteful of potential talent.

A basic belief in educational philosophy is that the difference of exceptional children is only one of degree: They are more like other children than unlike them. They must be treated first of all as children who need to express their individuality, and adjustments to their differences made within that framework. The label "exceptional" is only used in order to obtain a better understanding of the child. In times past, in their zeal to provide for exceptional children in need of special help, some educators overemphasized the label and forgot that the "children" part of the label is most important.

The manner in which exceptional children think, learn, and behave is not a different kind of behavior from that of other children. Even the degree of difference is not so great that it makes the child radically different from others. But the difference in degree is what

---

[1] Paul Witty, *Reading In Modern Education* (Boston: D. C. Heath and Company, 1949), p. v.

1

makes the child exceptional, whether this difference is in the learning or behaving level of the child.

"Exceptional" refers to children who differ from the average to an extent that their differences warrant some type of special school adjustment, either within the regular classroom or in special classes. It includes both those children whose differences make them unable to perform up to the level of the average, as well as those whose differences allow them to perform above the average. It includes the mentally and physically handicapped and the emotionally and socially disturbed as well as the mentally and physically superior. If exceptional children are different from the average, then the problem becomes one of determining how different a child must be before he can be called exceptional. It is not easily answered for any one of the specific areas of exceptionality, and is certainly unanswerable when applied to all of the diverse areas encompassed by the label "exceptional children."

State laws regarding the distribution of funds have perhaps realistically developed along the lines of test results using national norms. Within the local school itself, however, the determination of the need of special provisions for an exceptional child should be based upon whether or not the child is able to benefit to the limit of his ability from the existing classroom organization.

Identification

The purpose of any label is to aid in identification. In many areas, administration of exceptional children has only in the past few years moved from the "labeling" phase into the making of curricular adjustments. Because the steps to be taken following identification have not always been clear, the identification process itself has often encountered difficulties and been delayed. Only through identification, however, can awareness of problems be developed. Once the problem has become known, the pattern in American public education has been that solutions are not long in forthcoming.

A major American cultural problem has been the overuse of labels so that they become more than just terms meant to explain. Children have, in some instances, been "branded" with labels so that, instead of aiding in understanding, the label has dominated the general public's thinking about the child. Such terms as "gifted" and "talented" are currently enjoying great popularity. "IQ" was formerly a popular term. All areas of the physically handicapped have long had to resist the stereotyped public reaction to the labels "blind," "deaf," and "crippled." When there is reason to believe that a label will not aid in better understanding a child, use of it should be avoided.

In some ways, every child is likely to be exceptional. In keeping with current interest in the gifted, the Association of Childhood Education, International, published a booklet entitled, *All Children Have Gifts*.[2] It is true that exceptionality is not limited rigidly, and that all children do have gifts. The area of exceptional children merely supplements understanding about children, and should in no way replace other already existing areas.

Advances

The exceptional child has come to a higher level of acceptance and understanding in the last decade than ever before. One of the reasons for this change has been increased understanding of children generally, through research and observation. Of equal importance, however, have been other factors less directly concerned with the school itself than with social pressures.

Increased public concern for exceptional children, evinced in such successful lay-professional group movements as the National Association for Retarded Children, has focused more attention on specific groups of children. As would be expected, the parents of children whose exceptionalities are readily apparent have been able to move more rapidly and with more success than the parents of children whose exceptionality is less apparent. Parents whose children are mentally retarded, blind, deaf, crippled, or have speech problems have organized with professional people in movements to aid their children. Parents of the gifted and the perceptually handicapped, because these exceptionalities are less observable, have been less successful in their efforts, but the steady growth of the National Association for Gifted Children and other organizations are signs that these areas of exceptionality are making progress.

The increased attention paid to education as part of the current intellectual renaissance has resulted in additional government and

---

[2] Anne S. Hoppock, *All Children Have Gifts*, Bulletin No. 100, Association of Childhood Education, International, 1958.

industry support for academically talented students. Through the National Defense Education Act the government has become directly concerned with precollege training in science, mathematics, and foreign languages. This recognition of both individual differences and the necessity of making special provisions for these differences has come gradually. The emergence of the field of exceptional children has been the direct result of increased interest in providing for individual differences.

Widespread acceptance of the theory of individual differences has resulted not only in recognition of exceptional children, but also in the making of provisions for them within the framework of school programs. The extent to which school administrators have accepted the theory of individual differences can be partly measured by those provisions, which often are not special classes but provisions within regular classes. Denial of the existence of exceptional children is an unrealistic philosophy which most likely results in no better than a mediocre education for any child in such a situation.

The public school administrator has no realistic choice but to recognize individual differences. Recognizing them, he then has a commitment to provide for exceptional children in the best possible manner in that particular situation. This means acceptance and understanding of the special problems and needs of these children, and the support of differentiated instruction to provide for these needs.

Equal opportunity for all is a tenet basic in democratic beliefs. Equal opportunity for all, however, does not mean the same opportunity for all. It has wisely been said that "there is nothing so unequal as the equal treatment of unequals." Children are not equal in their abilities to learn, physical makeup, or temperament for learning. To provide the same education for all children, under the false assumption that this is democratic, would doom all exceptional children to a poor education. Differentiated education, in terms of the child's "unique nature and needs," is democratic because it provides for the fullest possible development of each child.

Special Education and the Exceptional Child

Special education is that part of education which deals specifically with the exceptional child. The role which special education plays in the education of exceptional children is often confused with the philosophy of special classes. Special education is concerned with the identification of and provision for children who are unlike the average, whether this be in the regular classroom, the special classroom, or in some combination of both. This is a broadened concept from that previously held which limited special education only to the education of those exceptional children who were assigned to special classes.

This broadened concept can be more fully realized when it is noted that "in 1948 one in ten [exceptional] children was enrolled in a special education program; in 1958, one in four was enrolled."[3] Actually, it is neither the goal of special education nor the philosophy of modern education to place children in special classes merely because they can be labeled in some specific way. The purpose of the special class is to make available a learning situation in which children who are unable to benefit to the fullest from regular classroom instruction can be successful. Differentiated instruction within the regular classroom is the necessary first step. When this is impractical or ineffective, consideration should be given to special class assignment.

Special education has developed as an area of study devoted to curriculum development, teaching techniques, identification and diagnosis, materials development, and teacher training for exceptional children. The field is concerned both with the exceptional child in the regular classroom and in the special class. Program development for exceptional children as a part of the total general education program has been stressed.

The program for exceptional children has not been seen as something which separates exceptional children from all others, but something to help the exceptional child to function effectively in an average world. The program for exceptional children is accepted as one part of the public school's total responsibility, not particularly for any specific group but a part of the dedication to the development of all children to the limits of their abilities. The program for exceptional children must not be fostered at the expense of other children; if that happens, it is doomed to failure. A wise program for exceptional children benefits all children. For example, special class

---

[3] Romaine P. Mackie and Patricia P. Robbins, "Exceptional Children in Local Public Schools," *School Life* (November 1960), p. 16.

programs for mentally retarded children benefits them by establishing more realistic goals, but at the same time it releases the regular classroom teacher from having to move so slowly with these children that she is unable to give adequate time to the remaining children in her room.

A major concern to those in special education is the emotional appeal often attached to certain areas of exceptionality. Where an appeal is based upon facts, and the goal is better understanding of the exceptional child, no harm is done. Often, however, when drives for funds utilize emotional appeal, misinformation concerning the particular area of exceptionality is spread. This type of program must be avoided for it results in the child having to overcome an incorrect public attitude toward him. His adjustment problems to an unexceptional world are great enough without added misunderstanding and misinformation.

Another concern is the "bandwagon" appeal of the area of exceptional children. Public interest does shift about, and when this interest results in the establishment of permanent, well-planned programs, it should be welcomed. But when public interest demands "crash" programs, designed merely to do something, the pressure should be withstood—crash programs are usually short-lived and unsuccessful. They often stand in the way of the establishment of permanent programs because everyone remembers how "we tried that once and it failed."

Scope of Monograph

It is the purpose of this monograph to present a general overview of what is known about the learning and teaching practices applicable to exceptional children. The term "exceptional child" covers a broad area, and even limited discussions of each area within this broad term still covers much material. This monograph is not intended to be definitive; it is rather intended to present the current thinking about each of the many areas to be discussed. Where the author is aware of disagreements, the disparate points of view will be presented. There is no doubt that some readers will disagree with the author's points of view—the monograph was not written with the intention that everyone should agree. Even the organization of the chapters will stimulate some disagreement, but in order to cover as many areas of exceptionality as possible the author has attempted what at this time he believes to be a logical treatment of the subject.

The area of mental exceptionality includes both those above and below average. The area of the slow learner, or child who is below average in mental ability, but who is not in the retarded range is a good example of the complexity of the problem. To most, the "slow learner" refers to the child within the IQ range of 75–90, but in some states (notably Ohio) "slow learner" refers to the child more commonly known as the retarded child within the IQ range of 50–75. Another monograph in the series will deal specifically with the slow learner, so that only the placing of him in the area of the exceptional, or briefly describing his characteristics, is sufficient here. The mentally retarded and the severely mentally retarded or trainable child are also discussed. The definitions of such children, their characteristics, and how they are identified are presented. Teaching practices found effective with these children and research dealing with their adjustments are discussed.

The bright, gifted, and "very gifted" are discussed at the other end of the continuum. Because the upper part of the continuum is currently receiving so much attention from both the general public and researchers, considerable attention is devoted to it.

The area of physical exceptionality recognizes that the child with superior physical ability is exceptional, but little attention is given other than to recognize that it is in this area that the child should be categorized. The physically handicapped by disease or injury are treated from an educational point of view, leaving the medical diagnosis and treatment for other sources. The cerebral palsied child is discussed as an educational problem. Partially and totally deaf and blind children are also discussed, as are children with speech problems.

The brain-injured child with perceptual handicaps is discussed. The proper placement of this frequently misunderstood child is conjectural. That he is a major concern to the area of exceptional children is clear, but there is disagreement as to how he can best be educated, even as how he should be categorized.

Another major area discussed is that of the socially and emotionally disturbed child. This is truly the newest breakthrough in cooperation between the disciplines of psychiatry, psychology, and education, for the proper education of these children must include planning from all three groups. The success of programs combining the efforts of these groups offers hope both for the recovery of these children and prevention of future emotional and social disturbances in children.

Children who are multiple-handicapped or exceptional in more than one way are discussed. More and more as our understanding of exceptional children develops are we aware that, in many instances, the label is applied only because a single area of exceptionality is noticeable. Once attempts are made to provide for that area in some special way, other areas of exceptionality emerge. The existence of special classes for the multiple-handicapped in virtually every large city is evidence of the extent of this problem.

Finally, the future of handicapped children is discussed. It is apparent that the exceptional child has at last gained recognition of his needs in childhood, but the need for adequate understanding and adaptations of his role as an adult is yet to be made.

CHAPTER II

Intellectual Exceptionality: The Below-Average Child

Intellectual exceptionality characterizes those children whose over-all intellectual capacity on existing tests indicates learning rates not within the average range. The implication is, of course, that the developmental rate of their learning capacity is above or below that of those in the average range. The deviation is commonly expressed in terms of an intelligence quotient, obtained on an individual test.

The distribution of IQ scores follows a normal curve. By definition, children whose composite IQ falls outside the average range are exceptional. It is with each of these groups that this chapter and the next deal—the severely retarded, trainable, educable mentally retarded, slow learners, bright, gifted, and "very" gifted.

The distribution of intelligence as determined by IQ tests is difficult to determine for a variety of reasons. Percentage figures differ for the number of children in each range of intelligence depending upon the number tested, the tests used, and the population being studied. Because the distribution of intelligence follows a normal curve of distribution, it can be stated with some confidence that there are about as many individuals in the above-130 IQ range as are in the below-70 IQ range. It was earlier thought that each of these groups included about one per cent of the general population, but estimates today usually put the figure at around 3 per cent. Close to 50 per cent are in the average range of 90–110 IQ; about 25 per cent in the lower half and 25 per cent in the upper half of the average range. More than 20 per cent of the population are in the 110–130 IQ range and more than 20 per cent are in the 70–90 IQ range.

There is general agreement among psychologists and educators that IQ test results are relatively constant, that they are fair predictors of academic success, and that individual tests are far more valid and reliable than group tests. Further, they make a valuable contribu-

9

tion to the understanding of an individual child when used as a measure of status attained and have fair value as predictors of future mental development. To read more into the test results is to make oneself susceptible to great error and vulnerable to criticism.

Assessment is most reliable with average children, least with mentally exceptional children, partly because of the very existence of larger groups of average children upon which to establish norms. The standardized testing procedure must, of course, be rigidly followed but certain cautions not covered in usual standardization directions should apply when assessing mentally exceptional children, perhaps when assessing all children:

1. The examiner should be a person familiar to the children. The classroom teacher should be well enough acquainted with the testing procedure to administer the test to her own children, if at all possible.
2. Testing should not occur before the children have become acquainted with one another and with the teacher.
3. The use of answer sheets separate from the test booklet itself is questionable with primary grade children of all levels of ability, and with children suspected of limited mental ability of all age levels.
4. The obtained IQ on a group test should be matched with that obtained on a different group test before the results are seriously considered as an indication of the child's potential. Even then, both for those far above and those far below average, the scores are only an indication that the child differs greatly from the average.
5. In cases where there is a great discrepancy between group test results or great variation from the norm, individual testing is advisable.

In identifying the intellectually exceptional child the group test is only an indication and a beginning, the first step in a screening process. Individual testing is a necessary next step.

Unfortunately, testing results currently depend more upon quantitative than qualitative factors. Adequate measurement of qualitative factors such as leadership, creativity, and motivation has until only recently been little more than discussed. Because current tests depend so much upon quantitative factors, assignment of children to special classes on that basis only creates many problems. In an effort to counteract the great dependency on quantitative intelligence test scores, most schools have insisted upon teacher observation and recommendation in addition to the I.Q. score before a child be placed in a special group. This should apply to special classes for retarded and for gifted children. Placement in a special program should be made on the basis that a special-class program will benefit the child more than the regular-class program.

It is unfortunate that the area of intellectual exceptionality is left so heavily to the mercy of test results. Teacher observation should be a valuable means of assisting identification; Gronlund and Whitney[1] report a study that corroborates this view. A pupil's judgment of his peers is emerging as another potential source of information about the mental abilities of the exceptional child.

Testing for intellectual exceptionality naturally directs itself toward two major categories—those of below-average capability, and those above.

The Intellectually Handicapped Child

The area of exceptionality dealing with children of below average intelligence for school purposes may be divided into the following categories:

1. Slow learner
2. Educable mentally retarded
3. Severely mentally retarded (trainable)

In spite of some confusion in terminology, no area of exceptionality is more clearly defined (with the possible exception of the physically handicapped) than that of the intellectually limited child. Paradoxically, this is true even though the definition is based on IQ, and the IQ concept itself is not so clearly defined.

For many years, "feebleminded" referred to children below 70 IQ. Within this group, those having 0–25 IQ were called "idiots," 25–50 IQ "imbeciles," and 50–70 IQ "morons." The very negative connotation of these labels reflects the attitude of that time toward such children and the hopelessness held for the educability of this group. These terms are outdated and should be avoided in all circumstances. Present-day definitions, based more upon educational prognosis than anything else, avoid negative connotations. They indicate the type of educational program which would be likely to produce the best results. The group earlier referred to as "morons"

---

[1] Norman E. Gronlund and Algard P. Whitney, "The Relation Between Teachers' Judgments of Pupils Sociometric Status and Intelligence," *Elementary School Journal,* Vol. 58 (February 1958), pp. 264–68.

are now called "educably mentally retarded," indicating that they are educable, even if to a limited degree. Those formerly labeled "imbeciles" are now termed "trainable," an obvious implication that lack of potential for school learning in the formal sense does not preclude the need for and the ability to benefit from training.

In addition to the educational terms "educable" and "trainable," another classification[2] used by the National Association for Retarded Children emphasizes social potentialities. The term "marginal independent" refers to the educable, "marginal dependent" to the trainable, and "dependent" to those who are totally dependent and hardly trainable.

A Manual on Terminology and Classification in Mental Retardation,[3] prepared by Heber in 1959 for the American Association on Mental Deficiency, presents an explanation of terms and classifications in the area of mental retardation. The manual includes definitions, medical classifications, behavioral classifications, and a glossary of terms.

How many intellectually limited children are there in the total population? It comes as a surprise to many people that half the total population is below 100 in IQ, or by definition below average. When one considers the extent of special concern given to the college-bound student and to the highly academic school program for all children, it is important to be reminded that more than half the children in the school population cannot conceivably achieve at this level. Attempting to state exact percentages of children in each IQ bracket raises problems: not all children have been tested; different tests may yield different results; and test results are often inconsistent.

Wallin, in an article entitled "Prevalence of Mental Retardates," lists sixty research studies on the prevalence of mental retardation.[4] Although many different methods of research were used on many different populations, it appears that roughly three per cent of the

---

2 National Association for Retarded Children, 129 East 52nd Street, New York, N.Y.

3 Rick Heber, "A Manual on Terminology and Classification in Mental Retardation," Monograph Supplement to *American Journal of Mental Deficiency*, Vol. 64, No. 2 (September 1959), pp. 111; Rick Heber, "Modifications in the Manual of Terminology and Classification in Mental Retardation," *American Journal of Mental Deficiency*, Vol. 65, No. 4 (January 1961), pp. 499–500.

4 J. E. Wallace Wallin, "Prevalence of Mental Retardates," *School and Society*, Vol. 86 (February 1, 1958), pp. 55–56.

total school population must be classified as mentally retarded. This agrees with the estimates of the National Association for Retarded Children. Of this group, two and one-half per cent could be labeled "educable," the remaining one-half per cent "trainable."

Slow learner. The term "slow learner" is sometimes used to refer to all children of below-average intelligence. In a few states it is used to refer to the mentally retarded. More commonly, those children who are below average in mental ability but not so low as could be called retarded are referred to as slow learners. They range in IQ from about 75 to 90. They are rarely adequately tested or even properly identified.

The objectives of teaching slow learners are less clearly defined than those for the retarded and trainable. This is another indication of the limited attention which has been given to this particular group of children. Slow learners are, unfortunately, too often expected to achieve at an average level, with little or no attention to and often with parental denial of the fact that the problem is more than one of inadequate instruction.

Quite obviously, slow learners cannot be expected to achieve as well as average children. Even additional effort often does not make the difference, although it is not uncommon for the highly motivated slow learner to achieve better than many children of average ability. The major objective, of course, is to aid the slow learner to recognize his limitations and his strengths, and to develop to the limit of his ability.

In the elementary school he is usually retained at least once. Research indicates that the retention is often of little value. With careful diagnosis and a thorough readiness and skills program, early retention should aid in avoiding some future problems. Delayed entrance into first grade, particularly when the child's birthdate is close to the cutoff date for entrance, is advisable.

The slow learner encounters his greatest difficulty in the language arts area, preferring to do things rather than talk about them. Not necessarily better in performance areas, he is able to see results for his efforts, and so prefers tasks in the nonverbal area. He is likely to be from a lower socioeconomic level. He is generally and incorrectly considered to be a child who does not try.

Although elementary school is not always enjoyable for the slow learner, because of the philosophy of grouping within the classroom at different instructional levels he is at least able to continue progressing, if at a slower than average rate. He becomes accustomed to being always in the slow group within the regular class. More often than not he is at the age of thirteen "socially promoted" to junior high school.

Adjustment to the junior high school is particularly difficult for the slow learner. Having to cope with many different teachers and unrelated subjects, and expected to operate at grade level, he experiences great frustration. Confronted with these among other numerous problems of adolescence, the slow learner frequently bides time until the age when he can drop out.

The slow learner makes up the greatest percentage of school dropouts and juvenile delinquents. He is the greatest behavior problem in the classroom. He shares with the gifted the dubious distinction of being the most neglected child in our schools. Clearly not college material, he has great difficulty meeting even the minimum standards of academic achievement set by most schools. Whether or not he ever receives a high school diploma usually depends more on the flexibility of the school's curriculum than actual achievement.

The slow learner perhaps more than any other child needs understanding. Because he is able to function in an average society, he needs to learn his role in such a world. This can only come from early identification, necessary curricular adjustments which will most likely include one retention early in the primary grades and possibly an added year in high school, larger blocks of time with fewer teachers in the junior high school, and a high school curriculum designed to teach him meaningful skills which will prepare him for his special role in life.

The slow learner in high school will benefit more by instruction in reading than from formal English classes. The material should be easy, designed to help him enjoy reading as well as to learn how to read better. Formal arithmetic instruction should be practical, involving as many real-life situations as possible. It will most likely not include formal algebra.

Whether or not he should be grouped with other slow learners will depend on many factors within the school. As an organizational plan, grouping slow learners has many advantages. In practice such classes are too often "dumping grounds," poorly taught and branded impossible situations. Sympathetic and understanding teachers in a school situation with a flexible curriculum which includes a work experience program for older students offers the best hope for the slow-learning child.

The educably mentally retarded child. As the label implies, "educable mentally retarded" refers to the child who can benefit from school, but only to a limited degree. His IQ falls within the 50–75 range. In academic achievement his highest attainment will likely not be much above the sixth grade level, and that high only when he has reached his full mental development. His learning rate and potential capacity is from one-half to three-fourths that of the average child.

Sarason[5] draws a careful distinction between mental retardation and mental deficiency. The truly mentally defective child, he indicates, cannot be changed. The implication to this is, of course, that mental retardation may be changed. Sarason quotes a study of Kirk's in which the term "incurability" is implied to be a part of mental deficiency but not necessarily a part of mental retardation. Sarason considers the diagnostic problem to be of primary importance. The following reasons which are given for attaching so much importance to diagnosis need to be carefully examined by all educators dealing with programs for mentally retarded children:[6]

1. Far too many lay and professional people still conceive of the diagnostic procedure as one primarily involving the use of psychological tests, a conception which overlooks the crucial importance of determining the nature and role of developmental factors, the current life situation of the individual, and the relation of these to the prediction of future level and quality of functioning.
2. It is obvious that the diagnosis of mental deficiency is a serious matter in that it has far-reaching implications for the individual and his family.
3. The diagnosis either of mental deficiency or mental retardation cannot be made by one professional specialist but by the teamwork of several. The psychologist, physician, social worker, and psychiatrist each have special skills which are necessary for obtaining the kinds of data on the basis of which a diagnosis can be made.
4. A diagnosis is communicated to parents whose lives have been, are, and will be affected by the fact that they have a defective or re-

---

[5] Seymour B. Sarason, "Psychosocial Problems of the Mentally Retarded," in *Psychology of Exceptional Children and Youth,* ed. William Cruickshank (Englewood Cliffs, N.J.: Prentice-Hall, Inc., 1955), pp. 440.

[6] *Ibid.,* pp. 442–46.

tarded child. Since in *every* case . . . the parents have played an important role in the child's development, just as the child has been an important factor in their lives, the communication of the diagnosis cannot be perfunctorily handled.

Studies of the characteristics of mental retardates as indicated by Magnifico[7] show that "the area in which the deviant comes closest to normalcy is that of physical capability." Such characteristics include:

1. Greater comprehension of the concrete than the abstract.
2. Reasoning power of mentally handicapped is limited.
3. Short attention span.
4. Limited power of association.
5. Unrealistic attitude toward society and themselves.
6. Lack of powers of self-criticism.
7. Limited judgment.
8. Lack of foresight.
9. Possession of a greater backlog of frustration experiences.
10. Satisfactory adjustment is not a characteristic of the mental retardate.

Any discussion of the characteristics of retardates would be incomplete without inclusion of the work of Johnson,[8] who notes that if his studies are supported by other research, the following educational implications could be made:

1. Mentally handicapped children should be reading at their Binet or Verbal M.A. level.
2. The *learning rate* of mentally handicapped children is at least *equal* to that of normal children of the same mental age of developmental level. The *rate* or *development is slower* for the mentally handicapped.
3. The evidence indicates that the mentally handicapped can generalize or transfer a principle better than normal children of the same mental age.

It is little wonder that the retardate frequently is not well adjusted when we consider how little understanding there is of this child. But

[7] Leonard X. Magnifico, *Education for the Exceptional Child* (New York: Longmans, Green & Company, 1958), pp. 129–33.

[8] G. Orville Johnson, *Comparative Studies of Some Learning Characteristics in Mentally Retarded and Normal Children of the Same Mental Age,* Syracuse University Research Institute, Office of Research in Special Education and Rehabilitation, 1958, pp. 114–15.

even with our limited understanding of the problems of the retardate, knowing that the child has limited mental ability is apparently a first step that has great value for, as Sarason has emphasized, "one of the major variables determining the quality of adjustment is the age at which the child's retardation was first noted."[9]

It is necessary to outline as clearly as possible the objectives of education for retarded children. The need to be specific is recognized, although most statements in the literature continue to be very general and often vague, and repetition of goals is apparent from one author to another as well as within a single listing. By making an analysis of the objectives for education of retarded children and restating the objectives "in terms of what the learner needs rather than in terms of what the teacher should teach" Stevens[10] has overcome these problems. He states the objectives or goals, which he intends to develop further in later publications, as:

1. Learning to maintain a state of physical well-being.
2. Learning to live safely.
3. Learning to understand oneself.
4. Learning to get along with others.
5. Learning to communicate ideas.
6. Learning to use leisure time.
7. Learning to travel and move about.
8. Learning to earn a living.
9. Learning to be a homemaker.
10. Learning to enjoy life through the appreciation of art, dance, and music.
11. Learning to adjust to the forces of nature.
12. Learning to manage one's money.

The administrative adjustments most often made for retarded children fall into several categories. Either because they have few retarded children or because of the particular philosophy of those in charge, some school systems prefer that all children be taught in the regular classroom. The arguments that this is more democratic, that the slow children are stimulated by the brighter ones, and that the slow children learn by listening are no longer seriously considered

---

[9] Sarason, *op. cit.*, p. 457.
[10] Godfrey D. Stevens, "An Analysis of the Objectives for the Education of Children with Retarded Mental Development," *American Journal of Mental Deficiency*, Vol. 63 (September 1958), pp. 234–35.

valid. Other reasons for not establishing special programs may be limited space or lack of availability of trained teachers. Too often the retarded child in the regular classroom either remains unidentified and therefore misunderstood, or takes too much of the teacher's time trying to learn things that he is not capable of learning.

The special school for the educably mentally retarded child never really reached the point where it was providing for any large number of children. Probably the special school idea never really became popular because it would be practicable only in a large metropolitan area, the transportation problem would be great, and never answered was the basic question: is it wise to isolate so completely children who as adults will have to withstand unaided the competition of an average world? The question apparently became one of partial or complete isolation, and the special class in the regular school (partial isolation) won out over the special school (complete isolation).

Heck[11] describes the "special center" for the mentally retarded child within the regular school. This special center is the homeroom special class, with freedom to use all shops or special facilities within the school as any other class would. Such classes participate in all activities of the school, as the regular academic classes do.

The special class within the regular school is currently the most common method of providing for the educable retarded children. These classes are usually set up with at least partial if not full state support. Enrollment in classes for the retarded is usually about 15, but the average daily attendance is below this. The classes usually are labeled primary, intermediate, junior high, and high school. The primary class includes children from chronological ages 6 through 10, while the intermediate class usually includes children from ages 9 through 13. The junior high class usually includes those adolescents who have been passed beyond the special class in the elementary school, but rarely includes the retarded child who for some reason was not in a special class in the elementary school. The development of programs at the high school level for the retarded child has been very slow. Most retarded children, if they ever reach the high school level, drop out upon reaching the legal age for quitting school.

There is still some controversy over the relative advantages and

---

[11] Arch O. Heck, *The Education of Exceptional Children,* 2nd Ed. (New York: McGraw-Hill Book Company, 1953), p. 336.

disadvantages of special class placement for retardates. Thurstone[12] reviews the research and reports on her study which found that retardates who were left in the regular class were achieving better than those placed in the special class. She points out the possible reasons for this, but admits preference for the explanation that, due to the limited number of places available in special education programs, teachers are often willing to keep in their rooms mentally handicapped children who are making even a small amount of academic progress.

Although classes of mentally retarded children are usually established with the upper IQ limit being about 75 and the lower about 50, by far the greatest number of children in such classes are in the 65–75 IQ range. The wide discrepancy between the abilities of children at the two extremes has caused a great deal of thought about changing the IQ limits of the mentally retarded group to be from about 60–80 IQ, or even above. The upper IQ limit of the trainable group would then be 60 instead of the common current usage of a 50 IQ as the uppermost score.

Wrightstone[13] designed a research study comparing the effectiveness of a two-track plan of educating retardates with the more traditional single-track plan. In the two-track plan, the high educable track contained those with more educational potential; the low educable track, those with less. The single-track plan contained all levels of educable retardates in one class. Comparing the two plans in a variety of ways, no clearcut support was found favoring one plan over the other.

Kirk[14] points out that three points of view have been expressed concerning the education of the mentally handicapped child. "Some allege," Kirk reports, "that the curriculum of the special class must be *different* in kind or quality as well as in quantity than that for the

---

[12] Thelma Gwinn Thurstone, *An Evaluation of Educating Mentally Handicapped Children in Special Classes and in Regular Classes.* Cooperative Research Project, Contract Number OE-SAE-6452, Project Number 168 of the United States Office of Education, 1959, pp. 2–4.

[13] J. Wayne Wrightstone, *et al., A Comparison of Educational Outcomes Under Single-Track and Two-Track Plans for Educable Mentally Retarded Children,* Cooperative Research Project, Contract Number 6908, Project Number 144 of the United States Office of Education, 1959.

[14] Samuel A. Kirk, "What is Special About Special Education? The Child Who is Mentally Handicapped," *Exceptional Children,* Vol. 19, No. 4 (January 1953), p. 138.

normal child." Kirk points out that these differences have not been clearly defined.

Without much personal reaction to the second point of view, Kirk states that some people allege that "a good child developmental program is good for both normal and subnormal children. Since a good teacher in any class adapts instruction to the level of learning of her children, that is all that is necessary for a special class program." The third point of view, which Kirk endorses, alleges that "the curriculum of the special class is largely a regular curriculum similar to that for the normal child, but that part of the curriculum and the teaching procedure is special, since the special aspects deal with methods and procedures adapted to the specific learning disabilities of the child which do not necessarily exist in the normal child."

In direct answer to what is special about special education for the child who is mentally handicapped, Kirk states:[15]

> The special education of the mentally handicapped includes much of the regular aims and purposes of the curriculum for the normal child, but in addition includes a special class organization, special materials, a special diagnosis, special clinical teaching procedures, emphasis on learning disabilities, more systematic instruction, more parent education, and more individualization of instruction. These are some of the procedures that make the education of the mentally handicapped *special*.

Because of the extended readiness period necessary for mentally retarded children it is important that the teacher of a regular primary class who has one or a few mentally retarded children or the teacher of the special class know about the learning pattern of the pre-school child. Readiness for fomal learning occurs for most children in the home or nursery school, but the retarded child is often of school age before he comes to the place in his development where he has mastered some of the simplest basic readiness skills. This places upon the classroom teacher the responsibility of providing the experiences and training necessary before formal instruction can possibly be successful.

At the chronological age of 6, when the mentally retarded child enters the first grade, his mental age will be between 3 and 4½. Using the common rule of thumb applied to the time when formal

---

[15] *Ibid.,* p. 142.

reading instruction should begin and readiness activities can be replaced, at the mental age of 6½, it is obvious that the mentally retarded child in the regular first grade presents many problems. His mental age is at least two and perhaps as much as three and a half years below that considered necessary for success with formal reading instruction.

In addition to providing them the necessary materials for readiness activities beyond those ordinarily available, teachers of retarded children must also be given guidance in sound readiness activities which will be meaningful. Describing how readiness for reading develops at home and at school, Monroe[16] brings the child's development of readiness through seven stages, the understanding of which is valuable to any teacher working with children whose development may be retarded.

Because of the special needs of retarded children, it is desirable that specially trained teachers work with them. One of the major factors which has been a detriment to the continued growth of special classes had been the scarcity of adequately prepared teachers. Recognizing this particular need, the federal government has made available grants for research and the training of personnel who will train teachers in the area of mental retardation. The effectiveness of the expenditure of these funds is clearly demonstrated by the increased number of teachers certified to teach mentally retarded children and the number of class units in existence. With the increased understanding of the retarded child, a better educational experience for the retarded child is guaranteed.

The training program for teachers of educably mentally retarded children contains the same basic requirements as that for teachers of elementary grades. Although there is disagreement among many educators as to the need for training and experience with average children, this author believes that the basic areas of child growth and development, methods and materials in the language arts, social studies, and arithmetic areas, and a general education in the liberal arts are needed as much by teachers of mentally retarded children as by teachers of average children. In addition to this training (which, incidentally should be on the elementary level regardless of the age level with which the teacher plans to work) the teacher of

---

16 Marion Monroe, *Growing Into Reading* (Chicago: Scott, Foresman & Company, 1951).

mentally retarded children needs special training. Understanding the characteristics and needs of mentally retarded children, the curriculum best suited to their needs, and teaching methods and materials specifically intended for this group of children are essential to the program of teacher preparation. Practice teaching with both intellectually average children and mentally retarded children is also strongly advised.

The severely mentally retarded (trainable) child. The severely mentally retarded child is, by definition, one whose IQ is below 50. In terms of potential learning ability, those between about IQ 30–50 are referred to as "trainable." They are not considered educable in the sense that they would be able to benefit from the formal school program.

A very small percentage of the total school population, but a problem not at all in proportion to its relative size, is the severely mentally retarded or trainable child. Consisting of only a fraction of one per cent of the school population (two or three such children per thousand) the trainable child poses unique problems to school administrators.

Cruickshank[17] clearly states this problem:

> In recent years there has developed an extension of special education which violates the concept of educability and which brings to the public school new responsibilities quite foreign to its history. Reference is made to the mentally deficient child, oftentimes called the "trainable child." The concept of trainability has been developed to remind educators and parents that this group of children exceeds the traditional concept of educability basic to public education.
>
> It should also be pointed out that there is considerable difference of opinion regarding the responsibility of the public schools to this group of children, although state after state has very recently delegated the responsibility to the schools. There is no difference of opinion regarding the state's ultimate responsibility. All are in agreement that the state must assume responsibility for the training, care and treatment of children with intelligence levels below 50 or 55. The difference of opinion revolves around the single point of the delegation of this responsibility to the public school as the community agency to do the training.

---

[17] William M. Cruickshank, "Current Educational Practices with Exceptional Children," in William M. Cruickshank and G. Orville Johnson, Eds., *Education of Exceptional Children and Youth* (Englewood Cliffs, N.J.: Prentice-Hall, Inc., 1958), pp. 45–46.

The trainable child is one who is not educable, one who cannot be expected to profit from formal education in the regular or special class of the school. Many states exclude the child who scores below about the 50 IQ level from public school. The problem then becomes one of determining what agency is going to assume responsibility for this child if the public schools do not. Cruickshank[18] suggests expansion of the residential school programs for the retarded child to the extent that they can supervise day care centers. Cruickshank believes that since the trainable child is going to need a program throughout his life, not just until he is somewhere between 16 and 18, the public schools are not in the best position to provide for him. He believes that more appropriate lifespan agencies should assume the responsibility for the trainable child.

Because of the very special needs of the trainable child, and the absence of the need to eventually integrate the child into normal, everyday social living, the special school in connection with or followed by the sheltered workshop seems most desirable. For those children unable to function in or be provided for in the day care program, residential school placement is necessary.

Goldberg's point of view differs from that of Cruickshank with respect to the responsibility of public schools for the school age trainable child. Goldberg believes that "the existing community agencies (including the public school) should coordinate their efforts and provide their services to the individual when needed. . . . However, during the school age no other agency is better equipped than the school to provide education and training."[19]

The problem of caring for the trainable child is a very great one. The adjustment of the child himself, however, is often not so great a problem as that of the educably retarded child. One of the reasons for this, of course, is that the limitations of the severely retarded child are so readily apparent to others that far less is demanded of him. The mentally retarded child, because his mental limitations are not so obvious, is constantly exposed to the pressures placed upon average children, which he cannot possibly hope to overcome. Actual emotional problems are far less likely to occur with the

---

[18] William M. Cruickshank, "Planning for the Severely Retarded Child," *American Journal of Mental Deficiency*, Vol. 61 (July 1956), pp. 3–9.
[19] I. Ignacy Goldberg, "The School's Responsibility for 'Trainable' Mentally Retarded Children," *Phi Delta Kappan*, Vol. XXXX, No. 9 (June 1959), p. 375.

severely retarded than with the retarded, partly because the severely retarded are less aware of even their own mental limitations as well as the protected environment in which they so often live.

The program for the trainable child includes the simplest kinds of activities involving self-care, safety, and readiness for some type of vocational placement where they will do harm neither to themselves nor to someone else. Under careful supervision and on routine tasks they have been found to be productive enough even to be partially self-supporting. The rudimentary skills of writing their names, counting to ten, and such basic reading as "stop" and "go" signs are attempted with varying degrees of success. A followup study by Delp and Lorenz[20] of a group of children with IQ's below 50 who had received special class training found that "a good percentage can actually perform tasks to earn money, and a few can even become partially or fully self-supporting."

Saenger[21] reported on the characteristics of home adjustment, use of community resources, working for pay, and planning for the future of 520 adults who attended classes for severely retarded children between the years 1929–1955. Considering the great mental limitations of these individuals, Saenger's findings were generally very favorable.

State residential schools exist for those children who cannot be provided for in day care centers. Where day care centers are not available, or where the extent of ability is so limited that the child cannot benefit from the day-care program, residential placement is necessary. Only Arkansas, Nevada, and West Virginia have no state residential schools. It is unfortunately true that most state residential schools are full, with waiting lists for admission. In many cases payment for the state residential schools is based upon financial ability of parents. An ever growing number of private residential schools also exists for the trainable child. Kirk, Karnes, and Kirk provide a list of residential schools.[22]

---

[20] Harold A. Delp and Marcella Lorenz, "Follow-up of 84 Public School Special Class Pupils with I.Q.'s below 50," *American Journal of Mental Deficiency,* Vol. 58 (October 1953), p. 181.

[21] Gerhart Saenger, *The Adjustment of Severely Retarded Adults in the Community: A Study of Former Pupils of Low I.Q. Classes Held by the Board of Education of the City of New York, 1929–1956* (Albany: New York State Interdepartmental Health Resources Board, 1957), p. 176.

[22] Samuel A. Kirk, Merle B. Karnes, and Winifred D. Kirk, *You and Your Retarded Child* (New York: The Macmillan Company, 1956), p. 157.

The status of public school provisions for severely retarded children is reviewed in Kirk[23] in a survey that contains the practices throughout the United States and provides a clear understanding of the various ways in which the needs of the severely retarded are being met.

Research studies in Illinois[24] and New York[25] have provided much valuable information about the severely retarded. Capobianco[26] summarizes these studies indicating the purposes of them and their findings.

Summary

Studies of mental exceptionality clearly indicate that in order to provide adequately for a child, some measure of his intellectual status is essential. It is certainly helpful to know the potential of the child whenever possible, but the use of intelligence tests to determine present status can be done with a great deal more certainty than using them to project into the future. The use of measures of intelligence, when interpreted wisely, can contribute greatly to the goal of providing for all children.

The area of the intellectually limited child is arbitrarily divided into slow learner, educable mentally retarded, and severely mentally retarded categories. Because of the great need for further understanding of the slow learner, a monograph in this series will be devoted entirely to that phase of exceptionality. The educably mentally retarded child is having many provisions made for him in the public school systems throughout the country. The severely mentally retarded child, although there is still much discussion as to the agency which should assume the responsibility for him, is gradually receiving more and more attention.

---

23 Samuel A. Kirk, *Public School Provisions for Severely Retarded Children* (Albany: Special Report to the New York State Interdepartmental Health Resources Board, July 1957).

24 H. Goldstein, *Report Number Two on Study Projects for Trainable Mentally Handicapped Children* (Springfield, Ill.: Vernon L. Nickell, Superintendent of Public Instruction, January 1, 1956).

25 C. O. Johnson, and R. J. Capobianco, *Research Project on Severely Retarded Children* (Albany: Special Report to the New York Interdepartmental Health Resources Board, 1957).

26 Rudolph J. Capobianco, "The Training of Mentally Deficient Children," in William M. Cruickshank and G. Orville Johnson, eds., *Education of Exceptional Children and Youth* (Englewood Cliffs, N.J.: Prentice-Hall, Inc., 1958), pp. 242-8.

CHAPTER III

Intellectual Exceptionality:
The Above-Average Child

The area of exceptionality dealing with children of superior intelligence can be divided into three categories: bright, gifted, and "very" gifted.

Just as in the case of the retarded child, the IQ has for many years been considered the only criterion by which mental superiority could be judged. Fortunately, the past several years has seen a decided shift away from this limiting definition, particularly with regard to the mentally or intellectually superior child.

The historical development of interest in mental superiority has been very interesting but discouraging. Only because we are currently in a period in which mental superiority is placed in a more favorable position can we look objectively upon these changes in attitude. The emerging intellectual renaissance is clearly marked by changes in the attitude toward individuals with superior mental ability.

Until the latter part of the nineteenth century, the child who demonstrated superior intelligence by his performance was highly favored. But publications in which insanity and genius were related appeared in the late nineteenth century, placing the child with superior mental ability in a most unfortunate position.[1,2] The confusion of the terms "genius" and "superior mental ability" contributed partly to this problem, as did the suspicion toward anyone who was "different" from the average. In 1928 Witty[3] challenged this use of the word "genius," differentiating "genius" from high IQ. Genius, he explains, is the product of drive, opportunity, and ability. The use of the expression "potential genius" might provide a partial solution

---

[1] C. Lombroso, *The Man of Genius* (New York: Charles Scribner's Sons, 1895).
[2] J. F. Nisbet, *The Insanity of Genius* (London: De LaNore Press, 1895).
[3] Paul A. Witty and Harvey C. Lehman, "Nervous Instability and Genius," *Journal of Abnormal and Social Psychology*, Vol. 24 (April-June 1929), pp. 77–90.

to the problem, although the term "gifted" seems to apply better. The term "genius" should be reserved for those who have achieved eminence by outstanding achievement. The child of very high intelligence should not be referred to as a "genius."

Since the development of the Binet-Simon Scales in France soon after 1900, intensive study of mental measurement has been in progress. Designed originally only to measure the potential abilities of children so that those who could not benefit from public instruction could be identified, the Binet-Simon Scales came into this country with the publication, in 1916, of the Stanford Revision. The obvious fact that these scales not only indicated those unable to perform at an average level but also identified those who were able to perform far above that expected of the average was immediately recognized.

Lewis Terman disproved certain of the negative preconceived notions about the mentally superior child, although his proof to the contrary did not completely dispel many of the superstitions surrounding the child of above-average mental ability. In a monumental work[4] covering a period of thirty-five years in the lives of 1500 individuals who scored in the upper ranges of intelligence, Terman produces evidence that clearly refutes the belief that high mental ability necessarily means concomitant deficiencies in other areas of development. Quite to the contrary, he showed that children with high intelligence are better adjusted, better developed physically, and excel in all other areas compared to children of average intelligence.

With the flood of new information about bright and gifted children, the 1920's saw the development of many programs which at the time were highly praised. Leta Hollingworth and Lewis Terman stand out as the pioneers in this movement. But, oddly enough, the 1930's saw a complete shift away from interest in the child of superior intelligence. Only the Major Work Program in Cleveland, Ohio[5] continued to exist. The advent of financial difficulties throughout the country might be blamed, but the real reasons went much deeper. In a clearly defined anti-intellectual sweep, the advances

---

[4] Lewis M. Terman, ed., *Genetic Studies of Genius*, Vols. I–V (Stanford, Calif.: Stanford University Press, 1921–59).

[5] Walter B. Barbe and Dorothy Norris, "Special Classes for Gifted Children in Cleveland," *Exceptional Children*, Vol. 24 (November 1954), pp. 55–58.

made in educating one part of the general population—those with intellectual superiority—were ended. Good and not-so-good programs alike were ended.

Truly the 1930's and 1940's were not the period of the intellectual. Any attempt to provide for these children was countered with the statement, "We tried that once and it failed." There was little popular support of anything for the above-average child; parents supported even that little with the tiresome cliche, "All I want is an average child." But confronted with the fact that an average child probably would neither go to college nor be in a profession, parents usually backed down somewhat.

The Education Policy's Commission's publication in 1950 of *Education of the Gifted*,[6] and the American Association for the Gifted's *The Gifted Child*,[7] edited by Paul Witty, in 1951 marked the beginning of a new era of interest in the gifted. The Education Policy Commission's 1961 publication *The Central Purpose of Education*[8] presents a radical departure from the philosophy of earlier decades with important implications for the gifted.

For a nation to worship the average to the extent that a segment of the population was made to suffer could not fail to create problems. Only by a highly traumatic experience could this attitude be changed. The Russians provided such an experience in 1958 when they placed Sputnik I in orbit. The attitude toward children with mental superiority has changed rapidly since that time—we are now in a period when the urgency felt by many to do something for the bright youngster actually endangers him. After so many years of lethargy, if not outright hostility, public interest in making all provisions possible for the intellectually capable child is at an all-time high.

Passow[9] has stated well the relationship of the program for gifted children to the program for all children: "More and more we realize that the problem of the education of the gifted is really the capsule version of all the problems of education."

---

[6] *Education of the Gifted* (Washington, D.C.: Educational Policies Commission of the National Education Associaton, 1950).

[7] Paul A. Witty, ed., *The Gifted Child* (Boston: D. C. Heath, 1950).

[8] *The Central Purpose of Education* (Washington, D.C.: Educational Policies Commission of the National Education Association, 1961).

[9] Harry A. Passow, from an address given at Ohio State University, Columbus, Ohio, summer 1960.

Bright Children

There is little agreement as to what a bright child actually is, except that he is a child whose IQ is not high enough for him to be called gifted, yet one who is sufficiently endowed with mental ability that more can be expected of him than could be expected of the average. Perhaps any clear-cut definition of the bright child would have to depend to a large extent upon the definition placed upon the gifted.

If one uses IQ figures to limit the group labeled as "bright," no doubt an IQ of 110 would be the lower limit. The upper limit would probably be determined by the lower limit placed upon the gifted group, varying from one system to another as IQ's of 120, 125, 130, and 140. In larger systems, the range of IQ's for the bright group would likely be between 110 and 130, sufficient to include roughly 20 per cent of the total school population.

It is interesting to note that Cleveland, Ohio, has classes called "enrichment classes" for bright children. The presence of such classes in Cleveland are due, no doubt, to the high degree of success of their classes for the gifted. The enrichment classes are for children who do not qualify for the Major Work Program for gifted children, but who possess a degree of intelligence sufficient to profit from a curriculum differentiated, but perhaps not to such a degree or even in the exact same ways of the Major Work classes, from that offered the average.

The label "academically talented" has come into common use in the past few years to refer to those children who can be expected to attend college and benefit from enriched experiences in high school as well as college. The term was used first by the Conference on Academically Talented.[10] Conant has explained that the "academically talented" includes about the upper 15 per cent of the high school population; it implies a lower IQ limit of about 115.

Most of the research on mental superiority has dealt with only the brightest children. Throughout the country, many of the programs for the "gifted" are in reality programs for "bright" children. If including bright children in such programs subjects them to aca-

---

[10]*Conference Report,* National Education Association Invitational Conference on the Academically Talented Secondary School Pupil, J. B. Conant, Chairman, February 1958.

demic demands beyond their capabilities, or interferes with the development of correct self-concept, the programs can be doing more harm than good. It is true, however, that in many instances the enrichment programs being offered the bright and gifted reflect a sincere effort to provide for individual differences.

The Gifted

"Gifted" has been defined in many different ways, but it generally refers to the upper 1–3 per cent of the school population, based on a standardized intelligence test. The most common cutoff point in terms of IQ is 130, this representing roughly the upper 3–5 per cent of the school population.

The term gifted has been used in a variety of different ways, many of them unfortunate. In times past it was applied to the child of above-average intelligence who worked hard—including effort as a part of the definition, however, presents many problems. Achievement in academic areas has also been used by some to indicate giftedness. This too is unfortunate, for it places some children in the position of having more expected of them than they are capable of doing, when they are already achieving close to the level of their potential. Conversely, it excludes those who have potential for higher achievement, but who for one reason or another are not achieving. The use of the IQ alone as a measurement of giftedness generates many problems, but it does avoid many of the problems inherent in a broader type definition.

A widely accepted definition of "gifted" is that adopted by the American Association for Gifted Children:[11] "The gifted child is one who is consistently superior in any worthwhile line of endeavor." This definition, stated by Paul Witty, must include also the potentially high achievers. An adaptation of that definition might be "The gifted child is one who has potential creative leadership in any worthwhile line of endeavor."

A major problem in establishing definitions is the danger that the measuring instruments may fail to recognize potential ability. But for other, broader definitions there is no objective way to measure giftedness—the concomitance of many superior physical and emotional traits with high IQ tends to add difficulty to any definition.

---

11 Paul Witty, ed., *The Gifted Child* (Boston: D. C. Heath and Co., 1951).

But as Kirk[12] states so clearly, "admitting that superior intelligence is only one factor in determining success, achievement, or contribution to society, it still remains a basic ingredient of what we call 'giftedness.' "

In a summary of the research on the characteristics of gifted children, the author[13] found that generally speaking there was close agreement with Terman and Oden's[14] findings. The gifted child is characterized as being in better physical condition and better adjusted socially and emotionally than average children. Fliegler and Bish[15] present a portrait of the gifted as indicated by the research. They stress the need for more study of "children in low socioeconomic environments, of the impact of personality and value concepts upon achievement, and of the interrelated variables in adjustment . . . in order to provide a delineated picture of the gifted child."[16]

It can be argued that the gifted child who is achieving well in school is in less need of attention than the child of high ability who is, for one reason or another, not achieving. Concern for the underachiever has in recent years gained great momentum. Because the potential contribution of the underachiever will be lost unless the school makes radical changes, educators have given more and more attention to this type of child.

Gowan[17] has described the underachieving gifted student on the basis of his research and that of others as:

1. The gifted underachiever tends to be self-sufficient and unsociable. He is, therefore, harder to reach, and harder to interest in social activities. He learns less from exposure to the normal socializing effects of his peers because he has less contact with them.

2. The gifted underachiever has identified less with his parents,

---

[12] Samuel A. Kirk, *Educating Exceptional Children* (Boston: Houghton Mifflin Company, 1962), p. 40.

[13] Walter B. Barbe, "Characteristics of Gifted Children," *Educational Administration and Supervision,* Vol. 41 (April 1955), pp. 207–17.

[14] Lewis M. Terman and Melita Oden, "Characteristics of Gifted Children," *Educational Administration and Supervision,* Vol. 41 (April 1955).

[15] Louis A. Fliegler and Charles E. Bish, *Summary of Research on the Academically Talented Student,* American Educational Association (N.E.A.) reprint of "The Education of Exceptional Children, *Review of Educational Research,* Vol. XXIX, No. 5 (December 1959).

[16] *Ibid.,* p. 416.

[17] J. C. Gowan, "The Underachieving Gifted Child: Problem for Everyone," *Exceptional Children,* Vol. 21 (April 1955), pp. 248–49.

who themselves seem to be less active than parents of overachievers, and less supporting of him and of his increased needs.

3. Because the gifted underachiever is less sociable, and because most teachers are overachievers, he tends to find fewer surrogate parental models among his teachers. This added lack of identification with an adult model makes his behavior still more difficult to influence.

4. The gifted underachiever seems to have fewer salable skills, either to offer for part time jobs, to bolster his economic situation, or to gain elegibility for college scholarship.

Occupational possibilities are limited because he participates less and hence is less well adjusted; college is lost because of his poor scholastic showing. As a result, it is harder for him to become independent of an unsatisfactory family situation, harder for him to gain a sense of worth and participation through his job, and harder for him to keep going in college. The combination tends to push him out of school into an economic market where his marginal skills are suited only to situations from which he derives little if any job satisfaction.

A major breakthrough in the area of creativity appears to be taking place. It has long been thought that "creativity" might be a better, or at least a different, measure of giftedness than the quantitative IQ score. For lack of any means by which creativity could be measured, little more than occasional reference to this concept was made.

Guilford[18] and MacKennon[19] have led the study of creativity among adults. Guilford[20] classified intelligence as cognition, memory, divergent thinking, convergent thinking, and evaluation. The work of Getzels and Jackson[21] on creativity and intelligence is highly provocative. Their studies of children high in creativity but not so high in intelligence, and of children high in intelligence but not so high in creativity, clearly indicates that the relationship between intelligence and creativity is not so high as had been thought.

---

[18] J. P. Guilford, "Traits of Creativity," in Harold H. Anderson, ed., *Creativity and Its Cultivation* (New York: Harper & Row, Publishers, 1959), pp. 142–61.

[19] D. W. MacKinnon, "What Do We Mean By Talent and How Do We Test For It?" in *The Search for Talent* (New York: College Entrance Examination Board, 1960), pp. 20–29.

[20] J. P. Guilford, "Three Faces of Intellect," *The American Psychologist*, Vol. 14 (August 1959), pp. 469–79.

[21] Jacob W. Getzels and Philip W. Jackson, *Creativity and Intelligence* (New York: John Wiley and Sons., Inc., 1962).

The Minnesota Studies of Creative Thinking have been reported on extensively. Since 1959, Torrance[22] and his associates have published more than forty reports on the progress of their work. *Guiding Creative Talent*[23] provides an easily understood practical application of Torrance's work in identifying and guiding creative talent.

There are three distinct administrative patterns used in providing for gifted children. These patterns may overlap, but in some situations they are distinctly separated. They are special classes, acceleration, and enrichment within the regular classroom. It must be pointed out that these are administrative policies and as such offer no guarantee that the gifted child is being cared for any better because of administrative decision to adopt them—regardless of the type of program adopted, the classroom teacher is still the key person in providing education for any child.

"Acceleration" is defined as making more rapid progress toward a goal. In accelerating a gifted child's program, however, the emotional and social adjustment of the child as well as his academic progress should be considered. Grade-skipping means bypassing a grade, taking the child out of his present grade placement. This must surely be the least desirable method of acceleration. Placing a child of superior mental ability in a double grade (that is, one in which he does the work of two grades) would seem to be more sensible in those situations where acceleration is advisable.

Grade-skipping was at one time the most widely practiced method of providing for gifted children. Its popularity in the 1920's was so great that undoubtedly many of Terman's findings were influenced by the large number of age-grade disparities among those children whom he studied. Although research continues to support that acceleration of up to two years at the time the student finishes high school does not produce the harmful results predicted by many, educators are nevertheless wise in being cautious about grade-skipping.

Early admission to the first grade is advocated by some.[24] At the

---

[22] E. P. Torrance, "Publications in Open Sources Related to the Minnesota Studies on Creative Thinking" (Minneapolis. Minn.: Bureau of Educational Research, University of Minnesota). Mimeographed.

[23] E. Paul Torrance, *Guiding Creative Talent* (Englewood Cliffs, N.J.: Prentice-Hall, Inc., 1962).

[24] Jack Birch, "Early School Admission for Mentally Advanced Children," *Exceptional Children*, Vol. 21 (December 1954), pp. 84–85.

high school level, carrying a larger number of courses and attendance at summer school are other means of acceleration. Grade-skipping as such is rarely practiced at the secondary level.

Participation in an advanced placement program, taking college courses while still in high school, is another high school method of acceleration. The argument in favor of acceleration most prevalent today is that it gets productive scholars into the professions at earlier ages. Research supports this argument, revealing that productivity has resulted at remarkably early ages.[25]

Special classes as a method for providing for gifted children is in greater favor today than ever before. As has been stated before, only the Major Work Program of special classes for gifted children in Cleveland, Ohio, survived the 1930's, a time when such programs were considered undemocratic procedure. The current status of the Major Work Program clearly indicates both the wisdom of the administration of the Cleveland Public Schools and the ability of the supervisory staff. The Major Work Program at the elementary school level selects children of IQ 125 and above to attend Major Work classes with other children of about the same age. Followup studies of the graduates of these classes clearly indicate that this has been a highly successful program for gifted children.[26,27] Starting programs but dropping them as the educational pendulum swings away results in an inferior educational program as well as wasted effort and money. The continuance of the Major Work Program partly accounts for the soundness of Cleveland's program today.

Another program for children at the elementary levels is demonstrated by the type at the Colfax School in Pittsburgh, Pennsylvania.[28] The Colfax Plan places gifted children in regular classes for half a day but in workshop activities exclusively for gifted children for half a day.

At the secondary level, elective courses have always worked out as a form of special class for students good in certain areas. Today,

25 Harvey C. Lehman, *Age and Achievement* (Princeton, N.J.: Princeton University Press, 1953).

26 Merle R. Sumption, *Three Hundred Gifted Children* (New York: Harcourt, Brace & World, Inc., 1941).

27 Walter B. Barbe, "A Follow-up Study of the Graduates of Special Classes for Gifted Children" (Unpublished Doctoral dissertation, Northwestern University, 1953).

28 Hedwig Pregler, "The Colfax Plan," *Exceptional Children*, Vol. 20 (February 1954), pp. 198–201.

however, the honor section and college preparatory curriculum have developed to such an extent that even the smallest high schools are attempting by means of organized special classes to offer a better education for their brighter children. To the degree that these programs are being carefully planned and specific goals established, they are being successful. Merely yielding to public pressure to do something for gifted children, however, is resulting in many programs that are little different from what already exists, if they are that good.

The special school idea has received a great deal of national attention, but few such schools have been established. New York City's Bronx School of Science[29] is an outstanding example of a school established for a specific purpose, and one that has been highly successful. Existence of such a school is practicable in large metropolitan areas, but not practical in smaller communities. Rickover,[30] apparently concerned only with the education of the intellectual elite, has proposed the establishment of 25 high schools for gifted students throughout the country. Recognizing only the need for achievement, and this only on the part of the very bright, Rickover's proposals have received little more than passing attention from those seriously concerned with the education of children.

If the term "enrichment" means good teaching, then enrichment is an essential part of any program and every regular classroom. If enrichment in the regular classroom, however, means the intentional differentiation of instruction, materials, and grades, then it can be labeled as a distinct method of providing for gifted children. Unfortunately, the term "enrichment" is today being used in an almost glib fashion to justify that something is being done for gifted children. Perhaps the strongest argument for special classes is that enrichment is neither understood by most people nor actually put into practice in many classroom situations. The arguments against enrichment in the regular classroom are that it imposes upon the already overburdened classroom teacher the responsibility for additional planning, and that it draws the attention of other children to

29 William Dutton, "Dr. Meister's Beautiful School," *National Parent Teacher,* Vol. 49 (June 1955), pp. 4–7.
30 H. G. Rickover, "A Size-up of What's Wrong with American Schools," *U.S. News & World Report,* Vol. 43 (December 6, 1957), p. 91.

the ways in which the gifted child is apparently different from them.[31]

One of the major problems facing education today is whether or not the establishment of special classes for gifted children, on much the same basis as those established for retarded children, is advisable. The problems of adequately answering this question presently seem almost insuperable, but with continued research in education and child development, answers will be forthcoming. At the present time the answer appears to depend more upon what is done within the regular class than upon the administrative setup.

The problem of the qualifications for a teacher of gifted children is an equally perplexing one. It is essential, of course, that the teacher of gifted children, like teachers generally, have an understanding of child growth and development, teaching methods, and materials in addition to mastery of subject content.

At the high school level, there can be no question but that the teacher must have broad and extensive training particularly in the area being taught. At the elementary level, however, both interest and training in the gifted seems to be particularly needed. Special characteristics needed include understanding of gifted children, flexibility, as well as better than average intelligence. It has been stated in all seriousness that the "teacher of gifted children does not necessarily have to have an IQ so high as that of the brightest child in the room but that she must have an IQ at least as high as that of the lowest child in the special class." Special training for teachers of the gifted is developing slowly.

The past decade has been marked by greatly increased attention to the gifted. Broadening of the concept of giftedness has been a major step, and the study of creativity stands out as a major development. But curriculum differentiation for the gifted has been the major development for the gifted. Fliegler has discussed the kinds of differentiated instruction currently being advocated for gifted students.[32] The extensive coverage of mathematics, science, English, social studies, and many other areas in publications of the N.E.A.

---

[31] Walter B. Barbe, "What Is Enrichment?" *School and Society*, Vol. 86 (May 10, 1958), pp. 222–23.
[32] Louis A. Fliegler, ed., *Curriculum Planning for the Gifted* (Englewood Cliffs, N.J.: Prentice-Hall, Inc., 1961).

Project on the Academically Talented Student also reflects this new area of concern.[33]

Very Gifted

There is little agreement and virtually no extensive research concerning children of extremely high intelligence. Possibly because there are so few such children, generalizations about those who score in the highest levels of intelligence cannot be made with complete certainty. Terman and Oden[34] point out that, although the attitude toward the child who is "moderately superior" has changed considerably, the "old prejudices [persist] with respect to children testing in the higher levels of the IQ range."

It is not uncommon even today to hear psychologists and classroom teachers state that there is a noticeable difference in appearances, personalities, and learning patterns between the gifted child and the child of extremely high intelligence. Terman devotes considerable discussion to subjects of IQ 170 and above.[35]

Because Terman's study is the only one that has included in any appreciable number subjects at the highest ranges of IQ (all of the students—47 men, 34 women—tested above IQ 170 on the Stanford-Binet test) it is of the utmost importance to our discussion to review his findings.[36]

> Many comparisons were made to discover how the subjects of 170 IQ or above differed from the gifted group as a whole. The results of these comparisons were more often negative than positive. Variables on which the high group and the total group of either sex differed significantly included age at walking, age at talking, and age at puberty; health as rated in 1922, 1928, and 1940; age at marriage, marriage rate, divorce rate, and fertility.
>
> The ratings on nervous symptoms and mental adjustment as of 1922, 1928, and 1940 were almost identical for the high group and total group with one exception: in 1940 a somewhat smaller proportion of women in the high group than in the total group were rated as "satisfactory."

---

[33] Charles E. Bish, Director, National Education Association Project on the Academically Talented Student, 1201 Sixteenth Street, N.W., Washington 6, D.C.
[34] Terman and Oden, *The Gifted Child Grows Up*, p. 282.
[35] *Ibid.*, pp. 282–95.
[36] *Ibid.*, pp. 293–95.

Ratings on social adjustment in 1922 showed no difference between the high group and the total group of either sex. On the social adjustment ratings of 1928, the high-testing subjects of both sexes made a less satisfactory record than the total group, the difference in the case of the women being statistically reliable. However, in extracurricular activities both in high school and college there was no appreciable difference between the high group and the total group of either sex. Moreover, the 1940 test of marital aptitude (which is largely a test of aptitude for general social adjustment) also failed to differentiate the high group of either sex from the total group. Everything considered, it appears that the subjects of highest IQ have been, on the average, about as successful as lower-testing subjects in their social adjustments.

The high group more often learned to read at an early age and were more accelerated in school. Reliably more of the high men than of total men graduated from college; among women there was a slight (though unreliable) trend toward less schooling for the high group. A large proportion of high subjects of both sexes received much less schooling than they should have had.

In school grades there was no appreciable difference between the high group and the total group in the four years of high school. In college, however, the proportion making an A average was more than twice as great as for the total group, and Phi Beta Kappa or Sigma Xi honors were about 40 per cent more common in the high group than in the total group. The most challenging fact in regard to scholarship is that about 25 per cent of the most gifted subjects have college records that are only fair to poor.

Men in the high group made a better showing in occupational status than did men of the total group; relatively more of them were in the professional class, and relatively more were rated in the top 20 per cent for vocational success. However, women in the high group did not differ appreciably from the total group of women in occupational status. Among both men and women of highest IQ there were individual subjects whose occupational histories were much less satisfactory than might have been expected from their intelligence ratings.

The parental background of subjects of highest IQ was superior to that of the total group, especially with respect to educational and occupational status. Moreover, the spouses of high subjects made a reliably better showing on the Concept Mastery test than did the spouses of the total group. It is possible that these two factors may have contributed to the greater success of the high group.

The characteristics of the subjects of IQ 170 and above would probably have stood out a little more clearly if the high group had been compared with subjects of 140 or 145 IQ instead of with the total group. Two additional circumstances have tended to blur the picture: (1) the fact that the high group averaged more than two and a half years younger than the total group, and (2) the fact that some subjects who deserved an IQ of 170 or higher were rated below this level because of inadequate top in the measuring instruments used in the original survey. However, even when generous allowance is made for these factors, it is obvious that subjects of highest childhood IQ are not sharply differentiated in adult life from subjects who tested considerably lower. On the average, those of highest IQ accomplish more and are equally well adjusted, but one cannot anywhere draw an arbitrary IQ line that will set off potential genius from relative mediocrity. Some of our subjects who have achieved most notably did not, either in childhood or in adult life, rate above the average of the total group in tested intelligence.

The only extensive study other than that by Terman was made by Hollingworth.[37] By means of case study reports, Hollingworth describes 12 children who tested over 180 IQ. She explains that this includes those children who might be found "one in a million." The observations that to Hollingworth seem most obviously to emerge from these brief summaries of educational history are five.[38]

1. Such children as are here presented constitute difficult educational problems from their entrance in school. The problems are not only those of the teachers and educational authorities, but they are, chiefly, perhaps the problems of the children themselves.

2. Depending on the solution of these problems, such children may either be well articulated to the work of school and society and thus their remarkable talents be socially capitalized, or they may, on the other hand, develop distaste for such activities, negativism toward social projects, and personal obstinacy and recalcitrance, perhaps accompanied by bitterness.

3. The advantages of early recognition, appreciation and, if possible, measurement are apparent in the study of this small group of exceptionally intelligent children. Although all were identified fairly early in their lives, there are very different degrees of adaptation to school and society, ranging from opposition and truancy, through indifference, to rapt and enthusiastic preoccupation. To a considerable extent these variations appear to have depended on the earliness of identification of the child's intellectual quality. The valuable services of surveys, guidance clinics, and school psychologists are clearly manifested in this group of cases.

4. The cases that have achieved most contented and socially use-

[37] Leta Hollingworth, *Children Above 180 I.Q.* (New York: Harcourt, Brace & World, Inc., 1942).
[38] Hollingworth, *op. cit.*, pp. 234–35.

ful adaptation are those in which parents, teachers, and principals have made prompt use of special gift identification, have sought educational guidance, have personally fostered and supervised the child's development and the solution of his adjustment problems, or have taken advantage of such experimental classes for exceptional children as the schools have offered at the time.

5. Among the cases herein reported the clearest ones of easy and useful adjustment occurred when the exceptional child became a member of an experimental group comprised of others of his approximate kind.

Summary

The area of the intellectually superior child is divided into bright, gifted, and "very" gifted categories.

The bright child is the one above average in general intelligence who will most likely continue on to college.

Those children identified as "gifted" score in the next higher range in mental ability. Their gift is only a potential one, however, and the extent to which they develop it will be determined by how effectively we can provide for them. Today more than ever before provisions are being made for gifted children. It is hoped that these provisions will be of a carefully thought out nature so that they may be permanent, rather than ephemeral gains brought about by hysteria over Russian scientific advances.

The area of the "very" gifted remains to be explored adequately. Other than the findings of Terman and Hollingworth, little is known about those children at the highest ranges of intellectual ability.

CHAPTER IV

Physical Exceptionality:
Visual, Hearing, and Speech Problems

The major physical exceptionalities discussed in this chapter are the sensory handicaps, which include the problems of the partially and the totally blind and deaf, and speech problems. The motor disabilities of the orthopedically handicapped (which includes victims of cerebral palsy) will be discussed in Chapter V, along with brief mention of those with superior physical development.

Physical exceptionality has been more clearly defined for a longer period of time than any other exceptionality. Attention has been directed for many years to the areas of the blind and the deaf. The first major acceptance of the responsibility for the education of the exceptional child came in the form of provisions for the blind which did not presuppose that blindness implied hopelessness. It quickly became clear, however, that programs for the totally blind could not meet the needs of those who were only partially blind. For them, special programs have been organized in recent years. The realization that the blind child could be educated, using special methods and materials, opened the door for special education of those afflicted with nearly every type of physical handicap. After the success of programs for the blind, deaf programs developed. Provisions for speech handicaps developed much later, but the prevalence of speech problems has made this program much larger than even those for the blind and the deaf.

All of the fifty states make legal provision for special education for physically handicapped children. Although the methods by which the states make such provisions for the handicapped vary greatly, it is apparent that there is general acceptance of the responsibility of the state to make provisions.

Discussions of the adjustment of physically handicapped children labor under many problems. It was at one time believed that more emotional problems were to be found among the physically handicapped than among average individuals. The very fact that the physically handicapped were objectively different from other individuals immediately caused many people to assume the presence of correlatively more adjustment problems.

Wright[1] discusses the "way in which a person with a disability copes with his social and personal connotations, these being aroused by the fact that the disability imposes certain limitations and is felt as a loss or denial of something valuable." She points out that the somatopsychological relationship, the "conditions that depend upon the interaction between the person and others,"[2] is centered around the belief that the person with a disability encounters difficulty from his expectation that he must perform in a certain way. Wright believes that there are "fewer psychological experiences peculiar to persons with physical disabilities than an offhand guess might indicate." She summarizes research on the somatopsychological problems of the handicapped and generalizes that "the findings do point strongly to the conclusion that most persons with physical limitations make about as good a personality adjustment as do the nonhandicapped."[3]

Blindness and Limited Vision

The number of blind in the total population, including both children and adults, is about two per thousand.[4] Thirty-five to 40 per cent of all children have defective vision, however.[5] The exact number of children who are blind can only be estimated (some children are either being given private tutoring in the home, or are receiving no training at all), but Kerby reported 3689 pupils in schools and classes for the blind for the school year 1945–1946. About 80 per cent of the children in these classes were either born blind or had lost their sight before they were five years old. Only about 40 per cent were totally blind or only had light perception.[6]

---

[1] Beatrice A. Wright, *Physical Disability—A Psychological Approach* (New York: Harper & Row, Publishers, 1960), p. 3.

[2] *Ibid.*, p. 3.

[3] *Ibid.*, p. 374.

[4] Leonard X. Magnifico, *Education for the Exceptional Child* (New York: Longmans, Green & Company, 1958), p. 287.

[5] Karl C. Garrison and Dewey G. Force, *Psychology of Exceptional Children*, 3rd ed. (New York: The Ronald Press, 1959), p. 143.

[6] Winifred Hathaway and Berthold Lowenfeld, "Teaching the Visually Handicapped," in Nelson B. Henry, ed., *The Education of Exceptional Children*, Part II, 49th Yearbook of the National Society for the Study of Education (Chicago: The University of Chicago Press, 1950), pp. 146–47.

The extent of the child's visual acuity determines whether he is classified as having normal vision, impaired vision, or is blind. The child is classified as blind if the corrected vision in his better eye is 20/200 or less. He is considered partially seeing if his corrected visual acuity is between 20/70 and 20/200 in his better eye.

The Snellen Chart is used to measure visual acuity. This is the familiar wall chart with the large **E** at the top and an increasing number of letters becoming smaller on each succeeding line below. The chart is placed twenty feet from the child. Each eye is tested separately. 20/20 vision in one eye means that at 20 feet from the chart the individual can see what, and as acutely as, the normal eye can see. The number to the left of the slanted line is the distance constant; it does not change for those who can see at all, however poorly. For example, 20/70 means that the child being tested can see at 20 feet what the average child can see at 70 feet. Only in cases of those children classified as blind, however, does the distance constant change—for such children to be able to see the chart it may have to be moved closer than 20 feet. For example, if the chart must be brought to within 5 feet of him before the subject can see it enough to read it, and even then he sees it only as well as normal eyes would see it at 200 feet, his rating is 5/200.

A variety of visual screening tests are used in schools. The Snellen Chart has been subject to much criticism, but it is still the most common test, as well as the most economical. Other tests, such as the Massachusetts Vision Test, the Bausch and Lomb Ortho-Rater, the Keystone Telebinocular, and the Sight-Screener, employ mechanical apparatus. They involve a high expenditure of money for the equipment, necessitate careful training of the examiner because of the detailed nature of the test administration, and they are not easily portable. With these disadvantages, they are justified over the Snellen Chart only for screening children in need of referral.

A valuable study by Foote and Crane[7] was conducted with the support of the National Society for the Prevention of Blindness, U.S. Children's Bureau, Division of Health of the State of Missouri, the St. Louis Board of Education, the Washington University School of Medicine, and the office of Naval Research to test the efficiency of various vision screening methods. More than 600 first grade

---

[7] Franklin M. Foote and Marian M. Crane, "An Evaluation of Vision Screening," *Exceptional Children*, Vol. 20 (January 1954), pp. 153–60, 180.

children and 600 sixth grade children were given complete eye examinations. The tests mentioned above were given to all the children, except that the Ortho-Rater and Sight-Screener tests, considered beyond their abilities, were not given to the first grade children. In addition, ophthalmologists gave all the children complete examinations. The results of each test were filed and not examined until all the tests had been given. The ophthalmological examinations were used as standards to determine "correct referrals," "over referrals," and "under referrals." Out of each 100 children in the sixth grade, the Ortho-Rater, the Sight-Screener, and the Telebinocular missed 6 to 8 children whom the ophthalmologists found to need care and referred 3 to 4 children who did not in fact need help. In the light of this under referral particularly, the study concluded that the reliability of these tests was questionable. The Snellen test for distant visual acuity and the Massachusett's Vision Test, it was concluded, are the best screening methods. These two methods were recommended by the Joint Committee on Health Problems and Education of the National Education Association and the American Medical Association in 1957.

It should be pointed out that any test of visual acuity measures the degree of vision a child has but in no way indicates the efficiency with which he uses the vision. Many emotional and environmental factors can influence the efficiency with which the child uses the vision he has, complicating plans for the child. Kerby[8] reported that among those children in classes for the blind, the causes of the blindness could be classified as follows:

CAUSE		FREQUENCY, %
1. Infectious diseases		13.8
2. Injuries		7.3
3. Poisonings		0.1
4. Tumors		4.6
5. General diseases		1.5
6. Prenatal origin		64.1
Hereditary	15.6	
Cause not specified	48.5	
7. Etiology undetermined or not specified		8.6

Assessment of the potential abilities and adjustments of the visually handicapped has necessarily been difficult. The Hayes-Binet

8 C. E. Kerby, *Causes and Prevention of Blindness in Children of School Age* (New York: National Society for the Prevention of Blindness, Publication 110, 1952).

Intelligence Test has for many years been the most valuable instrument for measuring the intelligence of the visually handicapped. Adaptations of other standardized tests which delete those items requiring visual skills often result in scores which cannot be considered valid or reliable because of the broken test standardization. Techniques for assessing the abilities, achievements, and adjustments of the visually handicapped need further research.

The education of the totally blind is very different from that for the partially seeing. The definition of both groups is primarily an educational definition; fortunately, they have not been interpreted so rigidly as have standards for other areas of exceptionality. The definition given by Hathaway and Lowenfeld[9] points this out most clearly. The partially seeing are defined as children who have a visual acuity between 20/70 and 20/200 in the better corrected eye, or who show a serious progressive eye difficulty, or who have seriously affected vision due to disease, or children who have some visual defect and normal mentality but will benefit by the special equipment opportunities in the partially-seeing class.

The label "sight-saving" or "sight conservation" classes for groups of partially seeing children in the public school is perhaps unfortunate. The purpose of such classes is not one particularly of prevention; it is to make special adaptations in materials for those children who because of visual handicaps could not progress normally using regular materials—the curriculum for the partially seeing is the same as that in regular classes. Such classes are quite in keeping with the philosophy of education which stresses the development of each child to the limit of his ability in terms of his unique nature and means.

It is estimated that only about one in every 500 children are in need of special educational facilities for the partially seeing.[10] Because of the limited number of children in need of them, such classes usually include more than one grade. Wherever possible, the preferred plan is to have the sight-saving class meet together to work on those activities requiring special materials, but for other activities the children will be with the regular classroom. A list of equipment for partially-seeing classes may be obtained from the National

---

9 Hathaway and Lowenfeld, *op. cit.*, pp. 130–36.
10 *Ibid.*, p. 137.

Society for the Prevention of Blindness, 1790 Broadway, New York 19, New York.[11]

Education of the blind is accomplished through private tutoring, Braille classes within the public school, or residential schools for the blind. The major purpose of these programs is to teach the blind child how to adjust to a seeing world. Blind children are taught to read and write in Braille. Because Braille reading is slow, the use of long-play phonograph records (talking books) provides a means of obtaining information more rapidly.

Abel[12] discusses various administrative and curricular adaptations for the visually handicapped. Blind children attend schools for normal children under the provisions of "cooperative" and "integrated" plans. In the cooperative plan, the blind child is enrolled in a special class with other blind children, but he goes into the regular classroom for a portion of the school day. In the integrated plan, the blind child is enrolled in the regular classroom, but available to him in another room is a teacher of the blind to whom he may go for specialized types of instruction. Another pattern by which blind children are educated is the so-called itinerant teachers service. Under this plan, an itinerant teacher serves blind children in a number of regular classrooms, often in a number of different schools. The need for pre-school training visually handicapped children is far greater than for normal children without visual handicaps. It was long believed that visual deficiency caused other senses to become strengthened—the blind, for example, were thought to possess heightened senses of smell and hearing. Research has not substantiated this belief. Obviously, because of his dependency upon other senses, the blind individual might pay more attention to them, but this in no way means that his hearing, say, is better than that of other people.

The American Printing House for the Blind (1839 Frankfort Avenue, Louisville, Kentucky) supplies materials for blind children. The American Foundation for the Blind (15 West 16th Street, New York 11, N.Y.) provides information and lends publications about the blind.

---

[11] *Ibid.*, p. 138.

[12] Georgie Lee Abel, "The Education of Blind Children," in William M. Cruickshank and G. Orville Johnson, eds., *Education of Exceptional Children and Youth* (Englewood Cliffs, N.J.: Prentice-Hall, Inc., 1958), pp. 304–16.

Hard of Hearing and Deaf

Little attempt is being made to establish test hearing norms designed to distinguish the child who is deaf from the one who is hard of hearing. Magnifico[13] states that "it is generally conceded that when a child has a hearing loss of 20 decibels or more in both ears he is considered definitely handicapped as far as normal educational environment in our public day schools is concerned." Afflicted children can be classified in terms of whether or not they have learned to talk. Using this classification, deaf children are those without naturally acquired speech when admitted to school. Hard of hearing children are those who have acquired the ability to talk but need special educational treatment. There are, of course, a large number of children who have some hearing defect but do not need special educational treatment.

Because there is no decibel-loss standard which distinguishes the deaf, the hard of hearing, or the child who has only a slight hearing loss, the numbers of people in each of these categories seem almost impossible to determine. Stevenson[14] states that "a deaf person . . . is one *who does not react* understandingly to spoken language. A hard of hearing person is one who reacts to spoken language understandingly, provided the source is brought within his hearing range either through a loud voice, amplification of sound, or through some other mechanical device." It has been estimated that 4–5 per cent of school-age children have some degree of hearing impairment. Only about one-half of one per cent are identified in the public schools.[15] There is every reason to believe that the number of deaf in the country is about equal to the number of blind.

Garrison and Force[16] have summarized the etiology of hearing defects:

1. Deafness nearly always has its origin in childhood.

2. In the vast majority of cases it is due to diseased conditions of the nose and throat and is therefore usually preventable.

3. The source of the trouble may be either (a) some chronic disorder of the throat, such as adenoids, enlarged tonsils, catarrh, etc., or (b) an

---

[13] Magnifico, *op. cit.,* pp. 303–4.

[14] Elwood A. Stevenson, quoted in Henry J. Baker, *Introduction to Exceptional Children,* 3rd ed. (New York: The Macmillan Company), p. 347.

[15] Magnifico, *op. cit.,* p. 304.

[16] Garrison and Force, *op. cit.,* p. 260.

acute infectious disease which involves the throat, usually scarlet fever, measles, or diphtheria.

4. Wax accumulations and injuries to the eardrum are occasionally causes of deafness.

Myklebust[17] points out that there are two critical variables in the psychological consequence of deafness: "the age of onset and the degree of the impairment." He describes four levels of hearing loss:

1. A loss of 30–50 decibels. It is pointed out that this is not a problem of socialization but one of "basic awareness and monitoring."
2. A loss of 45–65 decibels. The loss at this level clearly affects social intercourse. The scanning function of hearing is largely eliminated. The individual with this degree of hearing loss "experiences considerable detachment and seeks social relationship with others having a similar degree of deafness."
3. A loss of 65–80 decibels. A loss at this level makes "personal, social, and general environmental contact . . . difficult."
4. A loss of 80–100 decibels. Because of the extreme hearing loss, "the use of vision and taction is mandatory. . . ."

Myklebust[18] divides the age of onset into the following categories:

1. Prenatal or before two years. Apparently when deafness occurs at this early age, the child has many added problems. For this group deafness has the "greatest effect on ability to communicate, with implications for impact on personality and emotional adjustment. Basic psychological processes, such as identification, are disturbed."
2. From 2 to 6 years. If the child hears normally for the first two years of his life, he has some benefits verbally. When the onset of deafness occurs after five years, classification of *deafened* is used.
3. School Years. "Language function is well retained for interlanguage purposes and in other ways." Although special education is often necessary, ego development and general emotional growth are less problematical.
4. Early Adulthood. The age range is 18 to approximately 30. He points out that although basic personality patterns are not altered, "undesirable traits may be accentuated."
5. Early to Late Adulthood. This group includes those 30 to 60 years old. The greatest problem for this age group is retention of former occupational position.
6. Later Life. In this group "the basic effect of the deafness is viewed

---

[17] Helmer R. Myklebust, *The Psychology of Deafness* (New York: Grune and Stratton, 1960), p. 119.
[18] *Ibid.,* p. 120.

more in terms of increased withdrawal and isolation, increased insecurity, and emotional stress rather than as an effect on personality per se."

Silverman[19] supports the statements of Myklebust: "Children who are deaf before the age of three are not likely to retain normal patterns of speech and language. Obviously, from age three to five years on, the later a child has lost his hearing the more apt he is to retain 'natural' patterns of communication by speech."

Adapting psychological tests for the deaf is more easily accomplished than for the blind. If the deaf child has learned to receive directions and to communicate his responses, regular tests of intelligence, achievement, and adjustment may be used, although certain items on particular tests may not be suitable.

There are a number of ways in which deaf children of school age are being educated. Whatever the means, it is encouraging that, as Silverman notes, education is "universally available to all deaf children."[20] Residential schools for the deaf enroll the largest number of deaf children. Other deaf children are provided for in day schools or in special classes within the regular school. Education is available for deaf children at all levels, including college. Gallaudet College in Washington, D.C., is specifically for deaf students.

O'Connor and Connor[21] made a study of a group of 52 deaf children who had transferred before graduation from the Lexington School for the deaf into regular public or private schools. The purpose of their investigation was to determine what factors might determine the success or failure of such transfers. About half the group was unsuccessful. The results indicated that the deaf, in order to be successful in the integrated classroom, needed facility in the use of language and speech. It was found that "the percentage of deaf pupils in a special school or class for the deaf who are logical candidates for ultimate educational integration in classes for the hearing is small."

The education of the deaf child is no different from that of the average child, except that the deaf child must receive information

---

[19] Richard Silverman, "Clinical and Educational Procedures for the Deaf," in Lee Edward Travis, ed., *Handbook of Speech Pathology* (New York: Appleton-Century-Crofts, 1957), p. 392.

[20] *Ibid.*, p. 396.

[21] Clarence D. O'Connor and Leo E. Connor, "A Study of the Integration of Deaf Children in Regular Classrooms," *Exceptional Children*, Vol. 27, No. 9 (May 1961), pp. 483–86.

by other than the auditory sense and he will have more difficulty learning to speak because he cannot hear the sounds. Obviously a major part of his special education will involve speech training. Learning special methods to do this is part of the training for a teacher of the deaf.

One method of communicating taught to deaf children is the manual alphabet, a means of finger spelling. In the manual alphabet, specific hand or finger symbols represent each letter. In another method, sign language, a single position of the fingers or movement of the hand may represent an entire phrase or expression. It is not so rigid as the manual alphabet, and all kinds of local signs are developed for particular purposes the child may have need of in his environment.

Lip reading is a method by which deaf children are taught to receive communication. Some sounds cannot be detected by watching a person's lips so that comprehension of what a person is saying is often dependent not only upon reading the lips but upon interpretation of facial expressions and gestures. For this reason, the term "speech reading" is taking the place of "lip reading," implying reading a speaker's articulation, not just his lips.

The combination of manual and oral methods is being taught to most deaf children. By means of both speech reading and sign language, the deaf child is better able to learn. As with all other types of methods of teaching, the choice is not an either/or choice, but rather a combination of many methods.

There are far more people who are hard of hearing than there are deaf. "The educational needs of the hard of hearing child are different from those of the deaf . . . because he has the potential for learning speech, speech perception, and language by more natural means, primarily over the auditory system."[22] For the hard of hearing child adjustments in methods of instruction must be made, depending primarily upon the severity of loss and the age at which it was first identified as a problem. When his hearing loss is slight, merely seating the child in the position in the classroom where he can best hear is often effective. For a greater degree of loss, a hearing aid is certainly desirable. Mastery of speech reading may also aid him in operating with his handicap.

---

[22] Silverman, *op. cit.*, p. 429.

The hard of hearing child is shy and retiring. Missing much of the speech of those around him he is unable to understand their behavior. Silverman has pointed out that "The lower grades seem to be affected more than the higher grades, probably because of more oral instruction in the lower grades and greater dependence upon textbooks in the upper grades."[23]

The availability of diagnostic services for the deaf and hard of hearing, coupled with the increased amount of attention to the education of the deaf and the hard of hearing guarantees these children more hope. Medical, psychological, and educational research is constantly adding valuable information about them.

Speech

Because so much dependency is placed upon oral communication, even the slightest speech handicap is noticeable. The social pressure on every individual to speak as nearly like the "norm" as possible is extremely great. Because so much attention is given to correct speech, a child with a slight speech difficulty may develop a severe handicap as a result of the pressures and negative attitudes of those around him. Individual variations are barely tolerated— even pleasing-to-the-ear qualities such as certain regional accents are criticized solely because they are "different."

This great attention to so-called "normal" speech probably accounts for the generally accepted statement that there are more problems in the speech area than in any other of the areas of handicapped children. In attempting to determine the percentages of school-age children with speech handicaps, great variations are noted, estimates ranging anywhere from two per cent all the way up to an alarming thirty per cent.[24] There is obviously little consensus on what constitutes a speech handicap.

The area of study concerning the child with a speech handicap is highly developed, despite disagreement among educators within the area itself. The teacher or administrator is often handicapped by a lack of understanding of the terminology used in this area. Under the heading "A Glossary of Terms Frequently Used in Speech Path-

---

[23] *Ibid.*, p. 428.
[24] Magnifico, *op. cit.*, p. 312.

ology," Wood[25] lists and defines more than 400 terms in current usage. It can certainly not be expected that the school administrator or teacher will learn all of the specialized vocabulary common to the speech pathologist. A brief definition of certain general terms seems advisable, however. The terms "stuttering" and "stammering" are today used synonymously. "Functional" (or "psychogenic") speech defects are caused by psychological factors; they have no actual physical basis. "Organic" speech defects, on the other hand, are caused primarily by physical defects. A "decibel" is a unit in the measurement of loudness. "Aphasia" and "dysphasia" are synonomous, meaning a speech handicap due to a brain injury or disease. Kleffner objects to the terms "aphasic" and "brain-injured" being used synonomously. "The term 'aphasia' refers to a specific kind of deficit in language ability."[26] There are two types of aphasia: "expressive" and "receptive." A child who can understand what is said to him but cannot express his own thoughts in words is afflicted with expressive aphasia. A child who cannot receive or understand speech is afflicted with receptive aphasia. "Audiology" is the study of hearing. EEG stands for "electroencephalogram," a recording of electrical currents in the brain used to diagnose brain injury. "Speech reading" is the more recent expression for what was previously known as "lip reading."

There are a number of ways in which speech handicaps may be classified; because of great overlapping, however, these are at best only classifications for convenience. Speech handicaps may be classified either by causes, by symptoms, and as organic or functional. Ainsworth[27] classified speech problems under the following headings:

1. Problems of speech development
2. Problems of articulation
3. Problems of voice
4. Problems of stuttering

---

[25] Kenneth Scott Wood, "Terminology and Nomenclature," in *Handbook of Speech Pathology, op. cit.,* pp. 48–68.

[26] Frank R. Kleffner, "Teaching Aphasic Children," in James F. Magary and John R. Eichorn, eds., *The Exceptional Child* (New York: Holt, Rinehart & Winston, Inc., 1960), p. 331.

[27] Stanley H. Ainsworth, "The Education of Children with Speech Handicaps," in *Education of Exceptional Children and Youth, op. cit.,* p. 387.

5. Special Problems
   a. foreign dialects
   b. cleft palate
   c. cerebral palsy
   d. hearing loss
   e. aphasia
   f. laryngectomi
   g. stage fright

Retarded speech development affects 5 out of every 1000 children. The more common causes, according to Johnson,[28] are:

1. Mental subnormality
2. Illness or physical disability, especially during crucial periods of speech development
3. Lack of sufficient speech stimulation, as in homes where there is little or no vocal play with the baby or where the adults are relatively quiet
4. Oversolicitous parents who, anticipating baby's wishes, wait upon him so zealously that he simply experiences no urgent need for speech
5. Overly strict parents who punish the child who falls short of speech standards that are beyond his stage of development
6. Intense shock, fright, or shame

Delayed speech takes three forms, variously exemplified in the child who is able to talk but does not, the child who makes sounds but is not intelligible, and the child who has little or no speech.[29] At about 12 months a child should begin associating single words with objects. Between 18 and 24 months he usually begins making sentences.

Faulty articulation describes the greatest number of speech problems found in the elementary school. Lisping, the most common speech problem, is an articulatory problem. Lallation—in which the *r, l, t, d,* and/or *s* sounds are defective—is a problem of articulation. All other articulatory defects are called "oral inaccuracies," a wastebasket term for any mild articulatory defect.[30]

Voice or vocalization problems are generally classified into three or four categories. About one per cent of the school population present this type of speech difficulty.[31,32] Stuttering is sometimes in-

---

28 Wendell Johnson, "Teaching Children with Speech Handicaps," in *The Education of Exceptional Children and Youth, op. cit.,* pp. 183–84.
29 Ainsworth, *op. cit.,* p. 387.
30 Magnifico, *op. cit.,* pp. 312–13.
31 Johnson, *op. cit.,* p. 180.
32 Ainsworth, *op. cit.,* pp. 392–93.

cluded in this classification, although it is treated separately in this discussion. Pitch may be too high, too low, or monotonous. Pitch is determined by the size and shape of the larynx. For this reason, men tend to have lower-pitched voices than women. Every individual has a "natural pitch level." Failure to use one's natural level may "impair the effectiveness of his voice" or "damage his tone-producing mechanisms."[33] It is expected in our society that men will have deep voices (low pitch) and our women's will be higher. Attempts to change the natural pitch level, merely to conform to the dictates of society, raises great question.

The loudness or softness with which a person speaks should be determined by the situation in which he finds himself. When an individual inappropriately uses loudness or softness, or when he consistently uses one without regard to the situation in which he finds himself, he is considered to have a speech problem. This is particularly a problem of the hard of hearing child, unable to hear the loudness at which he is speaking. Inappropriate volume may also be a result of emotional strain.

Problems of pathology are usually grouped into four headings: nasality, breathiness, hoarseness, and harshness.[34] Nasality is caused by air coming through the nose rather than through the mouth. Breathiness is caused by too much air coming through the vocal chords. Hoarseness and harshness may be due to inflammation of the larynx and vocal chords.

Rate of speaking can be too fast, too slow, or "jerky."[35] The cause could be faulty speech habits or an indication of emotional strain.

The problem of stuttering is an extremely important one. About one per cent of the school-age population has this type of speech handicap, the sex ratio predominantly boys and ranging from 2:1 to 10:1, "depending upon age, grade, standards of investigation, and the like."[36] Although stuttering or stammering has been described as excessive repetition, a break in the rhythm of the speech, and so forth, modern research points to the belief that it is best described as a "deviation in the *fluency* of the speech."[37] Most stuttering develops between the ages of two and four. It has been pointed out

---

[33] *Ibid.*, p. 393.
[34] Johnson, *op. cit.*, p. 180.
[35] Ainsworth, *op. cit.*, p. 180.
[36] Garrison and Force, *op. cit.*, p. 294.
[37] Ainsworth, *op. cit.*, p. 396.

many times that under certain circumstances all people may stutter. Even the so-called stutterer does not stutter all the time: "probably close to 90 per cent at least [of the time], the stutterer is as 'fluent' as the person who does not stutter."[38,39] For this reason, it is important that the teacher identify only excessive lack of fluency in speech, excluding the occasional lapses which can happen to any individuals at any ages.

There seems to be little evidence to support those who believe that stutterers are different in some physical or constitutional way. It is commonly believed that stuttering is symptomatic of an emotional problem, but "study of large groups of stutterers through various personality tests and inventories, however, does not yield as definite findings in favor of the stutterer being psychoneurotic." A third view, that stuttering is a learned behavior, has stimulated research on stuttering as a learned response or its relationship to anxiety.

Each of the other special types of speech problems have specific diagnostic and remedial procedures associated with them. The speech program, for example, for the student with a foreign dialect will be quite different from that of the child with a hearing loss. The classroom teacher plays an important role in identifying children with speech problems. In the treatment of speech problems, the classroom teacher plays a supportive role. A specially trained speech therapist should be responsible for the remedial program.

There are a number of things the classroom teacher can do for the child with speech defects. Certainly when a speech therapist is available the teacher's role should be only one of supporting the specialist. Hahn makes the following suggestions for the classroom teacher:[40]

1. Recognize the nature of the speech defect
2. Keep records
3. Set a good example
4. Create a secure and pleasant environment
5. Manipulate the speaking situation

How much a classroom teacher will work with a child to correct a speech problem must depend upon both the teacher's training, and the severity of the problem and the emotional relationship between

---

[38] *Ibid.*, p. 396.
[39] *Ibid.*, pp. 398–99.
[40] Elsie Hahn, "Speech Defects," in *The Exceptional Child, op. cit.*, p. 317.

the teacher and the child. Activities with the class as a whole on articulation in voice problems may be helpful to individuals having problems within the class. Moreover, because we are so dependent upon the spoken word for communication, the concomitance of speech problems and emotional problems either resulting from or causing the speech problems are very common. The teacher must therefore consider the emotional sensitivity of the child with a speech problem. Heck[41] lists the following guiding principles for the education of children having defective speech:

1. Motivation: a child must realize the urgency for correction
2. Do not overemphasize the handicap
3. Diagnose carefully
4. Adapt exercises to defect
5. Eliminate worry
6. Educate in regular class
7. Avoid embarrassing the child

Within most public school systems, the itinerant speech therapist sees children for short periods one to five times a week. The speech clinic deals primarily with pre-school and adult therapy, but is able to provide a more thorough diagnosis for children of all ages than the itinerant teacher can provide. The effectiveness of the regular classroom teacher without specialized training as one who can correct speech problems and carefully supervise the speech therapy is highly questionable. Even should she be trained there is reason to question whether the teacher's role should be more than one of support for the individual or small-group work which the child gets with the speech therapist.

Research in the area of speech handicaps has been very extensive. There is a great overlapping of the classifications of various speech difficulties, which makes any research on causes or cures for specific types of speech difficulties difficult. The "multiple origin" theory is perhaps most strongly supported by research, as is individual "differentiated treatment."

---

[41] Arch O. Heck, *The Education of Exceptional Children,* 2nd ed. (New York: McGraw-Hill Book Company, Inc., 1953), p. 283.

Summary

In no area of exceptionality is a more extensive job being done than in providing for those children with visual, hearing, and speech problems. Even so, there are still many children handicapped in these areas who, if they are identified at all, are not being provided for in the best possible manner. It is very important to distinguish between the child with limited vision and the child who is blind, and between the hard of hearing child and the deaf child. The widespread need for speech correction work is recognized, but even with expanded services only a small number of those in need of help are being reached.

CHAPTER V

Physical Exceptionality: Orthopedically Handicapped, Health Problems, Superior Development, and Multiple Exceptionality

The areas of physical exceptionality discussed in this chapter—those involving the crippled, the child with health problems, and the child of superior physical development—and those discussed in Chapter IV are the chief areas of physical exceptionality of concern to special education. As research allows for more clear-cut definitions, new areas will undoubtedly be added, and some of the old ones will be of decreased importance if not eliminated as cures and preventive measures are discovered.

As intellectual exceptionality includes both those children of limited mental ability and those with superior ability, physical exceptionality should include the handicapped as well as those endowed with superior physical development. Included in this chapter is a discussion of the various phases of orthopedic handicaps and health problems. Little discussion is given to the child with superior physical development because in American society the athlete is given far more attention than any other type of exceptionality. The purpose of even including this group is to draw attention to the fact that this child also has special needs, of understanding, curricular differentiation, and protection from exploitation.

In no area is there so much possibility for lack of understanding as in the area of the physically handicapped, partly because in many instances the difference is not just one of degree. A child who is crippled, for example, must face not only the adjustments the average child must make, but additional problems of adjustment entirely different from those of other children.

Orthopedically Handicapped

The orthopedically handicapped child is one who because of injury or deformity does not have normal use of bones and muscles. It is virtually impossible to find any agreement as to how such children could be categorized. The term "crippled" seems to this author to apply best only to the orthopedically handicapped child. But many definitions of the crippled include those with health or medical problems, such as epilepsy and heart conditions, and it is recognized that because these two groups need similar training, there is justification for their being discussed together. The orthopedically handicapped will include those children suffering from cerebral palsy, polio, tuberculosis of the bones and joints, and congenital deformities.

Because of overlapping classification and, in some instances, disagreement, it is difficult to state the extent of the problem. As with many other areas of exceptionality, the figure of about one per cent is most often stated. Magnifico has said that "there is a total of approximately 600,000 crippled individuals under twenty-five in the United States. Studies indicate that 50 per cent of those cases of crippling can be cured entirely or in large part if they are discovered before the age of six."[1]

Heck points out four historical stages in the treatment of the physically handicapped, reflecting progressively better understanding and growing general acceptance of crippled children: extermination, ridicule, physical care, and education.[2] It is readily apparent that all phases of exceptionality have gone through about these same stages, with some areas at the present time only still in the stage of providing physical care.

Children in the orthopedically handicapped category are often found to be in the normal range of intelligence. The exception to this are children who have some injury or disease affecting the brain. They often are found to be in lower ranges of intelligence. The adjustment problems which orthopedically handicapped children

---

[1] Leonard X. Magnifico, *Education for the Exceptional Child* (New York: Longmans, Green & Company, 1958), p. 323.

[2] Arch O. Heck, *The Education of Exceptional Children*, 2nd ed. (New York: McGraw-Hill Book Company, 1953), p. 115.

face are gaining acceptance by others and accepting their own physical limitations.

Curricular differentiation is not so clearly defined for the orthopedically handicapped child as for many other areas of exceptionality. Individual instruction is frequently needed, and individualized approaches are used even in small group instructional situations. A developmental philosophy of teaching each child at his level is obviously essential.

Infectious diseases such as poliomyelitis and tuberculosis of the bones cause about a third of all orthopedic handicaps. Infectious diseases produce twice as many physically handicapped children as cerebral palsy does. The dreaded summer polio epidemics seem usually to strike under the age of six, boys more frequently than girls. The success of the National Foundation (formerly called National Foundation for Infantile Paralysis) in supporting research which led to the discovery of the Salk Vaccine is a measure of the value of continued research in all areas.

The length of time which orthopedically handicapped children remain in hospitals is becoming less.[3] More children with slight orthopedically handicaps are being better provided for in regular classrooms. Physical therapy is becoming more readily available. As with other areas of the handicapped, the trend is toward placing special classes within the regular rather than the special school. Although the special school program is not expanding as rapidly as the special class philosophy, reports of success achieved in special schools is most encouraging.

The educational program of the orthopedically handicapped child is little different from that of the normal child, with the exception that physical therapy and other aids are needed to help the child learn. There is need for close cooperation between medical professions and the teaching profession when working with orthopedically handicapped children. Physical adjustments must be made in the arrangement of the classroom, location of the classroom itself, use of equipment, and handling of supplies. The goal is, of course, to prevent his physical handicap from needlessly interfering with a child's educational progress.

---

[3] Frances P. Connor, "The Education of Crippled Children," in William M. Cruickshank and G. Orville Johnson, eds., *Education of Exceptional Children and Youth* (Englewood Cliffs, N.J.: Prentice-Hall, Inc., 1958), p. 440.

There are more than 500,000 cases of cerebral palsy in the United States. The cause of cerebral palsy is defect, injury, or disease before, at the time of, or after birth to that part of the brain which affects motor control. There is no cure for cerebral palsy, although treatment can help the child develop better motor control. Treatment includes physical therapy, occupational therapy, and speech therapy, all of which should be a part of the regular educational program of the afflicted child.

The educational problems which these children face are centered around activities which require fine motor control, notably writing and reading. Concomitance of other disabilities is very high—mental retardation exists in perhaps half of all cerebral palsied cases; speech and hearing problems are even more frequent.

Because the treatments for both are so similar, the current trend is to provide education and physical therapy for cerebral palsied and orthopedically handicapped children in common centers, often located within a regular school. The support of such programs is often a joint public school-community undertaking. Solving transportation, special equipment, and special instructional problems necessitates careful planning, but the results obtained justify all efforts.

Health and Related Problems

Primarily because of the Salk vaccine, there can be expected in the years ahead a decided decrease in orthopedically handicapped children. This is not so true in health and related problem areas, however. This classification includes many types of health problems, major among them being epilepsy, rheumatic fever, cardiac conditions, tuberculosis, allergies, glandular disorders, and diabetes. As medical science has discovered new and more effective drugs, children who formerly would not have lived are now able to lead somewhat normal, if restricted, lives. It becomes the problem of the schools to provide for these children proper education which will not in any way aggravate their physical conditions.

The various terms used to describe this type of child indicates that there is an awareness that he needs special education methods, but in no way suggests agreement on what they should be. Such terms as "delicate" and "lower vitality" merely indicate that special provisions are needed for them. Terms such as "delicate child" have almost passed out of existence. This may be due to the tendency to classify along more specific lines, as more is learned about children, rather than to group different types into larger categories. The "delicate child" was considered to be one whose physical condition was such that he needed a less strenuous school program than that offered in the regular classroom. On this basis, the category included children with heart conditions as well as those suffering from debilitations due to any physical illness or undernourishment. There was value in this classification for educators because it provided a grouping on the basis of the needs of the child, rather than on the cause of the disability.

Adjustments based on medical advice have to be worked out as to the best type of educational program for the child with a health problem. The normal work load frequently has to be reduced, although the curriculum itself is not different from that for other children. Whether the child can spend part of the day in regular classroom, will need homebound instruction, or a special class will depend a great deal upon the type and severity of the child's problem. The following summarizes well the type of program for these children:[4]

> Many of the children considered in this category can be taken care of to some extent in the regular public school classes, or in a combination program of regular plus special classes. . . . Sometimes, however, there are special schools and classes for these children, notably the open-air and open-window variety. It would be a sound idea that such children be supervised in school throughout the summer; otherwise, the progress made during the rest of the year might be negated. Frankly, in an urban quasi-automated society that prevails in the United States, the idea of the twelve months' school is wholesome for our children, healthy as well as handicapped.

All children who have had rheumatic fever do not necessarily have heart disease, although it is responsible for ninety per cent of defective hearts in childhood.[5] The symptoms of rheumatic fever are the same as those of generally poor physical health. For this reason, the classroom teacher should not hesitate to refer a child for

---

[4] Magnifico, op. cit., p. 333.
[5] Frances P. Connor, "The Education of Children with Chronic Medical Problems," in Education of Exceptional Children and Youth, op. cit., p. 500.

physical examination when he appears to be in poor health. The child who has had a rheumatic fever attack must spend a long convalescence in bed. A homebound teacher is a service that should be available to those children who are bedridden. Because such confinement is difficult for children, this period necessitates careful planning with the parent and the homebound teacher. Once the child returns to school, the greatest problem is "prevention of reinfection rather than limitation of physical activity."[6] If the condition is not serious, regular classroom is probably the best place for the child. In cases where this is not possible, the special classroom in the regular school seems advisable. The medical doctor will provide the school with information as to the type of program which the child needs.

Epilepsy

Epilepsy is a seizure, although not all seizures are epileptic. The terms "petite mal" and "grand mal," to describe the types of seizures, are still used today. The exact cause of epilepsy is not known, although it is strongly suspected that it involves an inherited predisposition to idiopathic seizures. Some physical disorder of the body, either due to brain injury or disease of some vital organ, may precipitate epilepsy. It is also thought that emotional upsets may be a precipitating factor. Most epileptic children can be provided an adequate education in the regular school classroom.

Heart Condition

Children with heart conditions are sometimes classified "cardiopathic." Whether the result is lowered vitality or other health problems, the cardiopath is sometimes grouped for educational purposes with orthopedically handicapped children. "This has been done not only because they are handicapped by a muscle defect (the heart muscle) but also because the general type of activity restrictions and curriculum adjustments which need to be made for them correspond closely to those for the orthopedically crippled."[7]

---

[6] *Ibid.*, p. 500.

[7] Lawrence J. Linck, Jayne Shover, and Eveline E. Jacobs, "Teaching the Orthopedically Handicapped and the Cardiopathic," in Nelson B. Henry, ed., *The Education of Exception Children, Part II*, 49th Yearbook of the National Society for the Study of Education (Chicago: The University of Chicago Press, 1950), p. 195.

So-called blue babies have heart defects which prohibit the proper circulation of blood, at one time considered incurable. Today, however, operations can make such a child nearly if not completely normal so that special educational programs may not be necessary.

The adjustment problems children with health problems face are often very difficult. One of the contributing factors is that the child with a health problem is frequently overprotected by his parents and teachers. Overprotection may be necessary because of the health condition but is often detrimental to his personality development. Another contributing factor is that the child with a health problem frequently does not understand his own limitations. Because he looks and acts like other children he cannot understand that he is denied the privilege of behaving as they do in certain situations. The development of good personal adjustment to a health problem depends largely upon thorough understanding of the problem by his parents and teachers as well as by the child himself. Careful medical advice as to the actual limitations of the child's behavior can contribute much to an attitude which will not result in overprotection.

Muscular Dystrophy

Muscular dystrophy has become known to the general public only in the past decade. Rather dramatic public appeals for research funds have met with generous response. Because muscular dystrophy has only so recently come to be generally known, any report of the incidence of this disease is naturally only an estimate, and likely to be low. There are about 200,000 victims in the United States alone, about two-thirds of them children.[8] The problem is obviously one great enough to warrant attention of medical research as well as educational planning.

Muscular dystrophy is a noncontagious disease which affects the voluntary muscles of the body. It usually strikes between the ages of two and five. His muscles gradually destroyed, the patient is eventually completely helpless. "Usually they do not die of dystrophy itself, but of complications brought on by other illnesses which the

---

[8] Elizabeth Ogg, "Out of the Shadows—the Story of Muscular Dystrophy," Public Affairs Pamphlet, No. 271 (New York: Public Affairs Committee, September, 1958), p. 2.

weakened muscles are powerless to combat."[9] There is known neither cure nor treatment for muscular dystrophy. Physical therapy provides little help because the disease is progressive.

The Public Affairs Pamphlet, "Out of the Shadows," presents the most complete, easy to read report on muscular dystrophy.[10] The discussion on the right of afflicted children to education is particularly pertinent to those in special education. It is recognized that for the child with muscular dystrophy schooling away from home is needed. Although the number of such children is relatively small and their potential contribution to society slight, special education must prepare each child to the limit of his ability, looking forward to that day when treatment, cure, and prevention will be discovered.

Superior Physical Development

It is surprising that superior physical development has rarely been considered a part of the area of special education. The extensive curriculum and personal adjustment problems facing those with superior physical development clearly indicate that part of the problem has been careful examined. The effect upon the child whose athletic prowess is exploited for the entertainment of society has been given little attention.

Superior physical development is no less important a gift than any other. It is almost foolish to state that the child so endowed might need special attention, for he has been made the victim of perhaps too much attention for many years. The importance of good physical health for all children cannot be minimized, but the development in America of physical education programs aimed primarily at turning the child with superior physical development into a star athlete, sometimes even at the expense of the minimum program for the average child, cannot be justified.

It is almost amusing to note that pleas for specialized programs for gifted children have not dared to go nearly so far as those for the athlete. At the college level, the athlete is sought out before he finishes high school, given numerous guarantees and inducements to attend college (whether or not they are legal). He is housed in a

---

9 *Ibid.*, p. 3.
10 *Ibid.*, p. 28.

special boarding house, fed special meals, required to keep certain hours, allowed to socialize only for specific lengths of time, and is given special tutoring whenever he encounters academic difficulties. To suggest that the same should be done for the intellectually gifted child is absurd, but if it is absurd for the intellectually gifted child, why is it not absurd for the child with superior physical development? To the extent that any program is harmful to him in his total development, it cannot be justified. Recognition that this phase of exceptionality is of concern to people in special education is needed.

Multiple Exceptionality

The term "multiple exceptionality" is used in preference to "multiple handicapped," even though the latter term is unfortunately in common usage. The author feels that attention needs to be given to those children who have more than one area of exceptionality in their makeup—to pay attention only to obviously handicapping features, so commonly done today, is to approach the area of multiplicity in a negative manner. Special education concerns itself with adapting the curriculum to meet the needs of a specific type of child. Because of our great emphasis upon single labels, we have often overlooked the facts that many physically handicapped children are mentally gifted, many mentally handicapped children are physically gifted. If special education is to concern itself with the below and the above average, and the author feels that it definitely must do so, a conceptual framework of "multiple exceptionality" must replace "multiple handicapped." Only if this happens will the blind child who is gifted have his gift recognized.

The purpose of a label is to help us better understand a child. Once he is given a label, however, it should not exclude other descriptive labels that might be applied to him. Preferably, perhaps, we should speak of "the gifted child who happens to be blind," but unfortunately the label seems to work in reverse—we hear often of the child that he is blind; only infrequently that he is gifted.

Unfortunately, classes are established for the multiply handicapped more out of administrative convenience motives than for the children themselves. Typically they are established because there are not enough children in any one category to justify a special class. They become a hodge-podge of unidentified or partly diagnosed problems. This is not to condemn entirely classes for the multiply handicapped in some situations, for they undoubtedly can serve a useful purpose. More than ordinary caution must be observed in establishing such classes, however. Putting many different kinds of problems together often only magnifies the problems of the children themselves.

Multiple exceptionality, on the other hand, seems to this author to be approaching the goal of all education—better understanding of each individual child. The goal is not the establishment of "multiple exceptionality" classes. The goal is to point out, for example, that starting special programs for a physically handicapped child is no reason to exclude him from a class for the gifted.

At least brief mention of the talented child must be made. Other than reference to the academically talented child, which is really only another way of saying the "smart child who does well in school," no mention has been made of creative ability in art, music, the dance, dramatics, and writing. Gifts in any of these areas are not any less important than any other kind of gift, but reference to them perhaps belongs in a discussion of "multiple exceptionality." These resources may be hidden in every child, only waiting identification and training. These talents may be found regardless of the mental level of the child or his physical condition.

The author does not mean to imply that there is no relationship between mental level and the ability to perform creatively in various areas. Research clearly shows that superior mental ability frequently goes with superiority in the talents. But every classroom teacher has known some exceptions—unable to perform well on tests of mental ability, they nevertheless were highly talented along some specialized line.

Even within intelligence itself there is such a wide range of abilities that it is quite possible for a child to be both mentally gifted and mentally handicapped. The "idiot savant" (an expression not widely used today) is a type of individual very limited in all mental areas except one, rote memory. The fact that his one ability was so strong usually resulted in his deficiencies being exaggerated. There are lesser, but real, discrepancies within the abilities of every child. Individuals who score very high on the total score of an intelligence test may have such decided deficiencies in certain areas that schoolwork may be extremely difficult for them. It is true that lack of interest in certain areas may account for some of the deficiency, but there is nevertheless a real weakness in ability that is only magnified by the lack of interest. Clinically, too great a discrepancy between areas may indicate emotional or neurological problems. But whatever the cause, multiple exceptionality within the area of mental ability frequently exists.

Not so extreme as the idiot savant but a great problem to teachers and administrators in the school situation is the child with uneven mental abilities. Placed in the gifted class, the child is usually unable to perform at a satisfactory level in his weak areas. This failure often results in his not being able to do well in his strong areas. In the regular classroom, the child is obviously far ahead of the rest of the class in certain areas and will exert great effort to resist being placed in the position where he must work in the areas of his weakness.

The child strong in the verbal areas stands the best chance of being identified in the schools of today. The child gifted in the nonverbal but only average in the verbal areas has little chance of being identified before the high school level, where he can elect his subjects. Unfortunately, IQ is not one but a composite of factors. The easiest child to teach and to provide for is the one whose abilities are all at about the same level, be it high or low. The child with widely disparate abilities presents much greater challenge to the school. The school needs to establish whether it intends to develop the child's strength or his weaknesses. For too long we felt it was the school's responsibility to work only on the areas in which the child was not up to the average. Fortunately, this philosophy is changing.

The perceptually handicapped child, the "Strauss Syndrome" type, perceives differently from others, and an emotional overlay is probably unavoidable. Because he is perceptually handicapped and emotionally disturbed the child can be said to be in the category of "multiple exceptionality." Because his perception is different from others, his verbal observations are sometimes creative—the term "bizarre" has frequently been applied to these responses. On several occasions pre-school children reportedly gifted have been found upon testing to be brain damaged. Their attempts at learning upon entering school were so nearly hopeless that parents' and neighbors' former classification of "giftedness" soon yielded to a more realistic term. A common example of this is the very young child, perhaps three years old, who is able to identify the model and year of many automobiles. Such ability at the age of three is phenomenal. But when the child is unable to learn how to read in the first grade, he almost immediately comes to be considered mentally retarded. The great change in the attitude of his parents and in the manner in which he is treated in itself may cause additional problems.

Because the brain-injured or perceptually handicapped child most likely has an emotional problem, probably as a result of his perceptual and conceptual difficulties, some educators feel that he should be treated first as an emotionally disturbed child. This would mean placing him in a class for emotionally disturbed children. It has been this author's experience, however, that this is not advisable.

Determining multiple exceptionality among the children who are physically handicapped presents problems when the area being investigated is intelligence. The handicapped child is often unable to perform the tasks on the usual standardized test because of his handicap or because he has not had the kind of experiences necessary in order to pass the test. Since the regular intelligence tests are developed on the assumption that all children have the same cultural and environmental backgrounds, which is certainly not true for physically handicapped children, the tests are extremely limited in their value with such children. Actual performance of the child in situations encouraging creativity in which adjustments have been made for his physical handicap is probably the best diagnostic measure of potential giftedness.

It is often said that the blind person's auditory sense is better than that of the nonblind person. It is thought that the blind person's hearing is actually no better than it would have been had he not been blind, but that out of necessity he learns how to use this sense to the utmost.

Hathaway and Lowenfeld[11] discuss a variety of areas in which the blind child is able to perform creatively. They recognize that drawing and painting are not possible for those who are blind, but they point out that modeling is an area in which blind children often excel and that "there is practically no instrument which the blind

---

[11] Winifred Hathaway and Berthold Lowenfeld, "Teaching the Visually Handicapped," in *The Education of Exceptional Children, Part II, op. cit.,* pp. 146–47.

child cannot learn to play—provided he has the necessary talent."[12] Often generalizations are made about one group of children without recognizing that the label "blind" is only one of the characteristics of this child. He may be exceptional in a variety of other ways, but the blindness itself does not make him either superior or inferior in any other area.

The presence of emotional problems among children who have disabilities is a major area of multiple exceptionality. Meyerson states that "the evidence on one point is clear. Children who have disabilities, as a group, tend to have more frequent and more severe psychological problems than others."[13] It can certainly be more than suspected that our attitudes toward handicapped children, perhaps aided by our failure to identify their gifts as well as the gifts of others, contribute to their multiple problems.

Some types of deafness are caused by nerve injury. It is not unusual that the receptive aphasic child is mistakenly thought to be deaf. It is not unlikely that some deaf or hard of hearing children actually have neurological involvements. The overlapping of these types of exceptionality make adequate diagnosis vitally essential if any educational program is to meet with success.

For some inexplicable reason, there has never been any relationship made by the general public between a speech difficulty and any particular level of intelligence. Other areas of handicaps have not been so fortunate, for "average" has been thought by many to be the highest functioning level of most exceptional children. Speech problems have been different, however, and have been treated very much as a physical problem which can be overcome. It is rather generally thought that stuttering is caused by emotional factors, as it well may be, but the general public rarely sees any need for treatment of more than just the symptoms.

When the area of multiple exceptionality is discussed, it is necessary to consider the relationship between emotional instability and mental superiority. It was for many years thought that insanity and genius were inseparable. Around 1900 this was carried to such an extreme that intellectual superiority in any form was actually shunned. Numerous examples of geniuses who became insane were

---

[12] Hathaway and Lowenfeld, *op. cit.,* p. 147.
[13] Lee Meyerson, "Somatopsychology of Physical Disability," in *Psychology of Exceptional Children and Youth, op. cit.,* p. 22.

frequently cited. That superior mental ability and insanity are necessarily related has been completely disproved. Terman's study[14] of 1500 gifted children proved that, far from being emotionally unstable, the gifted child was usually well adjusted—actually more stable than the average child. By means of a followup study, Terman showed that in the gifted group there was less incidence of instability than in the general population. There still remains the belief, and there is as yet no conclusive evidence to the contrary, that those extremely high in intelligence are more unstable than the average. It may well be that children at the extreme, the one-in-a-million variety, are not so emotionally stable as the average, when judged in terms of average standards.

Hollingworth[15] lists five adjustment problems which extremely bright children face in the early years of schooling:

1. To find enough hard and interesting work at school
2. To suffer fools gladly
3. To keep from becoming negativistic toward authority
4. To keep from becoming hermits
5. To avoid the formation of habits of extreme chicanery

While we agree with Hollingworth with the basic premise, statement of number 2 above would, in this author's opinion, be better expressed by saying that the gifted must learn to understand others less capable than himself, just as they must learn to understand him.

Summary

Physical exceptionality is perhaps the most important area of special education. Average efforts on behalf of the physically handicapped child will not be sufficient. If he is to be well-adjusted, it is imperative that his difficulty be adequately diagnosed early, and that special educational plans be made for him. To the extent that we fail to make provisions for the physically handicapped child, we are failing as educators.

In discussing the need for educational provisions for physically handicapped children, it must be recognized that limited resources as well as the small numbers of children with each type of handicap

---

[14] Lewis M. Terman, *Genetic Studies of Genius,* Vols. I–V (Stanford, Calif.: Stanford University Press, 1921–59).

[15] Leta Hollingworth, *Children Above 180 IQ* (New York: Harcourt, Brace & World, Inc., 1942), p. 299.

obviously make separate provisions impossible. Each case will have to be decided on its own particular characteristics, of course, but many disabilities can be provided for with a common educational program. Grouping these children in classes for physically handicapped children may be advisable.

The expression "multiple exceptionality" is offered as a better method of describing children different from the average in more than one way. In the author's opinion, the expression "multiple exceptionality" should replace "multiple handicapped." "Multiple handicapped" reflects the attitude that special education is concerned only with those children who have handicaps. The fact that most children with a handicap in one of the sensory areas are not handicapped in the mental area, and indeed may even be far above average, urges the need for a term which will not imply that a child handicapped in one area is incapacitated in all areas.

Multiple exceptionality is in keeping with the author's general philosophy that no child should be labeled for any purpose other than to aid better understanding of him. When a label becomes some kind of all-inclusive brand implying that because a child is like a certain type of child in one way he is necessarily like him in all ways, it serves only to his disadvantage. To the extent that the label does not help us in better understanding the child, we should not hesitate either to discard the label or substitute a more meaningful term.

It must be recognized that all children may be classified as "multiply exceptional." The very nature of children is to be different, in spite of the adolescent and even adult cultural standards which attempt to deny this physiological and psychological fact.

CHAPTER VI

Perceptually Handicapped and
Socially-Emotionally Disturbed Children

This chapter will discuss the perceptually handicapped child and the socially and emotionally disturbed child. In order to avoid any confusion, the author does not intend to imply necessarily that he believes there is any single cause, definition, or treatment of the perceptually handicapped and the disturbed child. The two topics are assigned to this chapter because they do not belong either in the sections on mental or physical exceptionality.

The reason for the necessity of clarification of viewpoint and the apparently needless attention to placement of these topics is that many perceptual handicaps and emotional disturbances foster similar problems, and many actually represent cases of multiple exceptionality. The author does not believe that perceptual handicaps necessarily cause emotional disturbance, but there is little doubt that many brain-injured children are also emotionally disturbed. This does not mean that the brain-injured must necessarily be emotionally disturbed, however, nor that the emotional disturbance is anything more than the result of lack of understanding of this atypical child. Nor does the author mean to imply that all or even many emotionally disturbed children are brain-injured, although some of them undoubtedly are.

In this chapter the author has tried to present the current thinking concerning the perceptually handicapped child in terms of definition and treatment. Disagreement exists in this area, and while the author has presented his opinion, he has tried also to present the dissenting opinions of others.

The socially and emotionally disturbed child occasions fewer disagreements than the perceptually handicapped among educators and psychologists, although there are still more unanswered than answered questions about cause and treatment. One point can be made in this area—there is universal agreement that more needs to be done.

Perceptually Handicapped

Perhaps the newest arrival in the area of exceptionality, not in existence but in identification, is the brain-injured child who is neither epileptic nor cerebral palsied. For too long this child has been called cerebral palsied, even if no gross motor impairment is evident. For want of another category, the label "cerebral palsy" is applied. It is, of course, true that the brain-injured child may or may not also have cerebral palsy, and that he may or may not be mentally retarded. The same conditions which cause him to be labeled "brain injured," namely an injury to the central nervous system itself, may also produce cerebral palsy, epilepsy or mental retardation. Alfred Strauss, a pioneer in the study of this type of child, preferred to classify such children as "brain injured with mental retardation, brain injured with motor handicap (cerebral palsy), brain injured with behavior disturbance, and so on."[1]

Various classifications for this type of child have been made. Referring to the given types of mental deficiency, Strauss set forth the differences between "exogenous" and "inogenous." The term "exogenous" came to be synonomous with the term "brain-injured child."[2] Others preferred to use the expression "brain damaged, CNS (central nervous system) impairment." The problem is apparently one of terminology. Stevens and Birch suggest the term "Strauss syndrome."[3] Strauss reports that on the basis of his research, these basic deviations in the mental makeup of brain-injured children exist:[4]

1. Disturbances in perception
2. Disturbances in concept formation (thinking and reading)
3. Disturbances in language
4. Disturbances in the emotional behavior

---

[1] Alfred A. Strauss, "The Education of the Brain-Injured Child," in James F. Magary and John R. Eichorn, eds., *The Exceptional Child* (New York: Holt, Rinehart & Winston, Inc., 1960), p. 137.

[2] *Ibid.*, p. 136.

[3] Godfrey Stevens and Jack W. Birch, "A Proposal for Classification of the Terminology Used to Describe Brain-Injured Children," in *The Exceptional Child, op. cit.*, p. 148.

[4] Strauss, *op. cit.*, p. 139.

Strauss referred to these as "brain-injured children," but there has been a great deal of controversy about that label. The argument runs that merely because a child behaves in this way does not prove brain-damage, and moreover all brain-damaged children are not characterized by this type of behavior. For this reason, Stevens and Birch[5] suggest the term "Strauss syndrome" to describe the brain-injured child displaying the perceptual and conceptual difficulties described by Strauss. Indeed, any label other than "brain-injured" that will provide better understanding for this particular type of child should be adopted. Whether or not one agrees that new terminology is absolutely necessary, the results from accepting a different label which in no way changes either those children who are put into this category or the procedures being developed hopefully to benefit them seems to be the only sensible course of action. One cannot help but wonder why in education, in which there are so many overlapping terms making sweeping generalizations about the types of children to be included, there should have developed such sensitivity about the use of the term "brain-injured." If this is the first sign of more careful diagnosis and delineation of various types of exceptionality, then the trend is indeed a good one. With this understanding in mind, one can refer to those children with no motor involvement he would have formerly called "brain-injured" as "perceptually handicapped" or "Strauss syndrome."

The number of children with brain injury is not known, much less the number of those who would fit into the Strauss syndrome category. It has been estimated that the number of children suffering from brain injuries is 2–5 per 1000. However, it is not unlikely that all individuals suffer some slight brain damage as the result of the perils of everyday living, which consists of falls, bumps on the head, and an almost continuous parade of small accidents.

There is every reason to believe that the number of brain-injured school children reaching school age is on the increase. In times past, most brain-injured children did not survive early infancy because of an inexplicable predisposition to respiratory ailments. With penicillin and antibiotics, what formerly was usually fatal to the brain-injured child is now little more than a normal illness. There are many who feel that the incidence of Strauss syndrome children is

---

[5] Stevens and Birch, *op. cit.,* p. 148.

much greater than generally suspected. This does not mean that all of these children are in need of special education, but some of the learning difficulties earlier classified as due to poor teaching or lack of readiness may in reality have been cases of the Strauss syndrome.

Information in textbooks about this type of child is conspicuous by its absence. However, the abundance of recent research on children of the Strauss syndrome type reported in the periodical literature is overwhelming evidence, perhaps, that the Strauss syndrome type of child is coming more to be recognized as another type of exceptionality. The increase in the number of groups concerned with perceptually handicapped persons indicates the increased interest in this area of both lay and professional people.

The diagnosis of brain injury is of course a problem for the neurologist, but the type of child described in the Strauss syndrome can rarely be detected by a gross neurological examination, however. There are cases where examination reveals no positive signs of neurological impairment, but because of many characteristic behavior patterns a diagnosis can still be made with a fair degree of certainty. In instances such as these, supportive psychological examination results are absolutely essential in the diagnostic stage. Whether this comes as a part of the diagnosis or after it makes no great difference, provided that it is not omitted. In any event, thorough psychological examinations of all children suspected of having neurological handicaps is essential for educational planning.

The role the educator plays in the diagnosis of brain injury may be one of referral. Unless suspected brain injury is clearly established by a neurologist's diagnosis, educators refrain from using this emotionally loaded expression. Brain injury is something from which a child never recovers, for brain tissue has been permanently destroyed. Other parts of the brain may be trained so that the damaged areas are perhaps bypassed, but cautious use of the term is nevertheless absolutely essential.

It is important that educators and psychologists be aware of the fact that the child being described is not necessarily mentally retarded. It is true that he manifests many of the characteristics of the retarded; particularly, he does not make normal progress in academic school subjects when taught by regular methods.

For a number of reasons, many children with brain injury are not identified until they enter school. What has until that time been labeled merely a behavioral problem soon becomes a severe learning problem. The school's responsibility in making a referral to the family physician is to describe those behavior patterns and the nature of the child's learning difficulties as clearly as possible. It will probably be the responsibility of the family doctor to refer the child for a neurological examination. If a school psychologist is available, preliminary referral to him will add additional evidence to support the teacher's observations.

Brain injury or damage can occur in the prenatal stage, at the time of, or after birth. The damage may be the result of an actual blow to the head or to any condition which would reduce the supply of oxygen to the brain for a length of time sufficient to cause permanent damage. Excessively high fever is a common cause of brain injury; birth injuries, perhaps, cause the greatest number of brain injuries. When the characteristics revealed by neurological examinations are congruent with those described by Strauss, as opposed to epilepsy or cerebral palsy, the child is said to be of the "Strauss syndrome" type.

The best current definition of brain-injured children is that given by Strauss himself:[6]

> The brain-injured child is the child who before, during, or after birth, has received an injury to or suffered an infection of the brain. As a result of such an organic impairment, defects of the neuromotor system may be present or absent; however, such a child may show disturbances in perception, thinking, and emotional behavior, either separately or in combination. These disturbances can be demonstrated by specific tests. These disturbances prevent or impede a normal learning process. Special educational methods have been devised to remedy these specific handicaps.

Strauss groups the characteristics of brain-injured children into three categories: perception and perceptual disturbances, thinking disorders, and behavior disorders. He describes perception as "an activity of the mind . . . between sensation and thought," a "means by which the individual organizes and comes to understand the phenomena which constantly descend upon him."[7] The Strauss syndrome child does not perceive a picture as a whole, each part

---

[6] Alfred A. Strauss and Laura E. Lehtinen, *Psychopathology and Education of the Brain-Injured Child* (New York: Grune and Stratton, 1947).

[7] *Ibid.*, p. 28.

identified in relationship to it. Rather, he perceives the individual parts separate from the whole. He also has great difficulty separating foreground and background in visual perception. Strauss showed that perception difficulties exist in the visual, tactile, and auditory fields. Perseveration, the inability to shift, is the consistent repetition or continuance of an activity once begun. In thinking disorders it has been found by numerous research studies that the brain-injured child is inclined to give bizarre responses. He is distracted more easily by unessential and accidental details. The child with the Strauss syndrome is inclined to want things in an exact, never-changing order—Strauss refers to this as a "formulistic" arrangement. Behavior disorders in the Strauss syndrome include such things as short attention span, high degree of distractibility and emotional shallowness. The child's "uncontrollable drive and disinhibition" are perhaps the outstanding characteristics which cause behavior problems in school.

The area of great disagreement over the Strauss syndrome is the fact that there is so much overlapping of classifications. There are those who feel that the Strauss syndrome is not a distinct type of exceptionality, but rather a combination of emotional disturbances, mental retardation, and cerebral palsy. The author's experience with learning difficulties leads him to believe that this is a distinct category greatly in need of further understanding and research.

Strauss found the brain-injured child who was not mentally defective characteristically to have great learning difficulties in school, in spite of proven normal intelligence.[8] On such tests the normal brain-injured or Strauss syndrome child scores higher in the verbal area than in the non-verbal. Particular strengths seem to be in vocabulary or word meaning, with decided deficiency in verbal reasoning areas. Eye-hand coordination activities are usually failed as are perception of items involving figure-ground tasks.

An excellent book that explains the "Strauss Syndrome" child is *The Other Child*[9] by Lewis, Strauss and Lehtinen. A section dealing with the education of the brain-injured child in the 1955 edition of

---

[8] Alfred A. Strauss and Newell C. Kephart, *Psychopathology and Education of the Brain-Injured Child*, Vol. II: *Progress in Theory and Clinic* (New York: Grune and Stratton, 1955), 266 pp.

[9] Richard S. Lewis, Alfred A. Strauss, and Laura E. Lehtinen, *The Other Child*, 2nd ed. (New York: Grune and Stratton, 1960), 148 pp.

the *Psychopathology and Education of the Brain-Injured Child*[10] is particularly valuable. Special techniques for teaching such children developed at the Cove Schools are carefully outlined. Whether or not the specific techniques are employed, a variety of activities are presented which should be helpful to the classroom teacher in working with any type of child who needs a different approach to learning. A good teacher will, of course, necessarily have to make adaptations to meet each individual case.

The brain-injured child is often placed in a classroom for the mentally retarded if he is unable to score high enough on an intelligence test for enrollment in the regular grades. The danger obvious in this type of placement clearly indicates the need for placement to be made on the basis of more than just an IQ score. Because of their behavior and perception problems, few Strauss syndrome children will be able to score high enough to indicate a potential above that of the retarded classes. But this should not justify assignment to such a class. It has been clearly demonstrated that many such children have potentials higher than previously thought.

Placement in a class for the mentally retarded may not necessarily be harmful, providing the teacher understands this type of child. However, the goal of the teacher in the mentally retarded class is to stimulate the children to the highest level of performance. This is accomplished by providing opportunities for many activities, a wide variety of materials, short periods on individual topics, and much stimulation. The brain-injured child, however, needs to have extraneous stimuli removed. A rather rigid pattern of instruction is strongly recommended, with as little change in the routine as possible. It is possible that the Strauss syndrome child could be educated along with the mentally retarded, but it is this author's opinion that the best instruction for both groups of children is not likely to be achieved in an integrated classroom.

As a result of work in Montgomery County, Maryland, Cruickshank[11] and others recently published a major contribution to the area of teaching brain-injured and hyperactive children that provides much practical information on programming and teaching

---

[10] Strauss and Lehtinen, *Psychopathology and Education of the Brain-Injured Child, op. cit.,* p. 28.

[11] William M. Cruickshank, Frances A. Bentzen, Frederick H. Ratzeburg, and Marion T. Tannhauser, *Teaching Methodology for Brain-Injured and Hyperactive Children* (Syracuse, N.Y.: Syracuse University Press, 1962).

methodology. They placed stress on the regulation of the school environment by means of a rigid time schedule, specific assignments, and follow-through on work expected. The success of the teaching situation was judged in terms of the academic progress of the children.

Residential school placement for the Strauss syndrome child is extremely expensive, and there are only a limited number of places where actual provisions are made for this particular type of child. In those cases where behavioral problems are so great or environmental conditions make remaining in the home inadvisable, residential placement may be necessary. Whenever possible, the child should be provided for in the regular public school, and for the first three grades preferably in special classes. From the fourth grade on the child who is mentally retarded should be directed to the mentally retarded class. The child with normal intelligence might be fitted into the regular classroom. There is an increasing number of school systems recognizing this problem and making special provisions for these otherwise extremely difficult-to-handle children.

In a comparison of brain-injured and non-brain-injured mentally retarded children, Gallagher asks:[12]

> Are the differences that can be seen between these two groups substantial enough to create recognizable differences in the total patterns of the development of children in these groups? The writer believes that this study and previous research direct an affirmative answer to this question. A second crucial question might be: Do these differences imply the need for drastically modified education and training programs or merely slight modifications in existing programs? Here the answer is less clear and depends to a large degree on which brain-injured children you are talking about. The range of different problems and lack of problems within the brain-injured group is large enough to cast considerable doubt on the notion that plans can or should be made for brain-injured children as though they were a homogeneous group.

Gallagher's study and others indicate that when the child with the Strauss syndrome is adequately diagnosed and taught by a teacher who understands his particular learning needs, he may be able to function effectively in classes for the mentally retarded.

---

[12] James J. Gallagher, *A Comparison of Brain-Injured and Non-brain Injured Mentally Retarded Children on Several Psychological Variables*, Monographs of the Society for Research in Child Development, Inc., Vol. XXII, 65, No. 2, 1957.

Placement of a Strauss syndrome child incorrectly diagnosed as mentally retarded in a special class with retarded children can be extremely harmful. But the Strauss syndrome children of normal intelligence will definitely need special educational adaptations. Because the number of these children will not be exceedingly great, the author believes that integrated classes including children of the educable level up to and including those of normal intelligence would be most sensible.

Socially and Emotionally Disturbed Children

Socially and emotionally disturbed children are maladjusted to the society in which they must live. The classifications are certainly not consistent, and there is a tendency to classify both emotionally and socially disturbed children as one group. The author prefers to define the socially disturbed child as one who is maladjusted in his relationships with others; the emotionally disturbed child, as maladjusted in his relation to himself. It is not unlikely that both characteristics might be found in the same child, but the reason for distinguishing between the characteristics is that they are not *necessarily* combined. The socially disturbed include such groups as juvenile delinquents; the emotionally disturbed include neurotic and psychotic children who may or may not behave antisocially.

In spite of continuous dinning about the relative frequency of mental illness, few attempts even to estimate the number of emotionally and socially disturbed children have been made, perhaps for lack of classification but certainly for lack of criteria for maladjustment. There is no question but that the figure is larger than the one per cent figure which seems to apply to so many other areas of exceptionality. But whether it should be two, five, or ten per cent or higher remains purely a matter of conjecture. Actually, if the figures were to include those children who would at any time throughout their childhood go through a period of severe "maladjustment," it is not unlikely that the number would include all children. The preponderance of socially disturbed boys as compared with girls is greatest in the elementary grades. Beyond the elementary school level, there seems to be more social maladjustment among girls than is found earlier.

Basic human needs of all individuals include ego status, social status, and physical and mental health.[13] To deny to a child any of these three may produce a situation leading to maladjustment. It cannot be said that the denial of these basic human needs always creates maladjustment, for overcompensation in a highly acceptable social manner may make up for the absence of one of these basic human needs. "The determinence responsible for emotionally disturbed behavior are to be found in the three categories: biological, psychological, and social."[14] There is great overlapping of these factors; it may be impossible to separate them when studying causitive factors.

By biological factors, Garrison and Force[15] mean physical conditions. This monograph has dealt with children who are basically different from other children. These differences, particularly when adequate provisions are not made for the child's development of selfconfidence in other areas and acceptance and understanding of his physical limitations, may lead to social and emotional maladjustment. It is apparent from research that social and emotional disturbances are more prevalent among the handicapped than the non-handicapped group.

Psychological factors deal primarily with the individual child's reaction to his environmental situation. These factors will be determined primarily in the child's own home, in his developing relationships with his parents and siblings. The manner in which he is reared by his parents will be of major importance. The effect of social pressures influencing adjustment have until recently been given little attention.

Social attitudes are probably the most obvious factor in adjustment. Whether the child is a member of a minority group, on the basis of race or religion, or whether his economic background makes him different from other children and places pressures upon him, detrimental effects may result from this social pressure. Other social effects, such as the social pressure to be like other children exerted on the child who, because of environmental or physical reasons cannot be like others, may also contribute to maladjustment.

---

[13] Paul Witty, "Reading Success and Emotional Adjustment," *Elementary English*, Vol. 27 (May 1950), p. 281.

[14] Karl C. Garrison and Dewey G. Force, *Psychology of Exceptional Children*, 3rd ed. (New York: The Ronald Press, 1959), p. 474.

[15] Garrison and Force, *Psychology of Exceptional Children, op. cit.*, p. 474.

The social pressures upon a child to achieve beyond his capacity is another factor to be considered.

The characteristics of the socially and emotionally maladjusted child include, among other things, lower academic achievement. Obviously, "the higher the school grade, the greater the differences between the emotionally disturbed child and the rest of the class." Emotionally disturbed children score lower on IQ group tests, but on individual tests they score about the same as the average. Interestingly, Bower[16] reported that "emotionally disturbed boys exhibited greater dissatisfaction with self in their school behavior than the other boys. Emotionally disturbed girls showed less dissatisfaction with self than the rest of the girls in the class."

It was thought at one time that various types of emotional instability might be related to various types of body builds. Meyerson points out that variations in physique might cause disturbances in some children but ". . . there is universal agreement that variations in physique need not necessarily lead to emotional handicaps."[17]

The reason the socially maladjusted and the emotionally disturbed are so frequently treated as one problem is because most often one goes along with the other. The types of symptoms of maladjustment and disturbance which the classroom teacher might look for are:[18]

Aggressive	*Retiring*
1. Lies constantly	1. Overly sensitive
2. Cheats	2. Daydreams
3. Steals	3. Tries overly hard
4. Destructive	to please
5. Cruel	4. Easily frightened
6. Bully	5. Overly selfish
7. Arrogant and defiant	6. Lives in a world
8. Frequent temper tantrums	of fantasy

Physical factors which should be noticed are nail biting, facial twitching, twisting hair, chewing clothing, picking at body (nails,

---

16 Eli M. Bower, "A Process for Identifying Disturbed Children," in *The Exceptional Child, op. cit.,* p. 348.

17 Lee Meyerson, "Somatopsychology of Physical Disability," in *Psychology of Exceptional Children and Youth, op. cit.,* p. 19.

18 Walter B. Barbe, "Locating Children with Emotional Problems," *Childhood Education,* Vol. 30 (1953), pp. 127–30.

nose, blemishes); weak, high pitched voice; rapid, nervous speech; selfconsciousness.

A number of factors impede the development of public school programs for the emotionally disturbed child. Perhaps the most important reason is the clear understanding that any program or class for emotionally disturbed children must include cooperative and continuous planning on the part of educators, psychologists, and psychiatrists. There is little rapport in many communities between all of these groups. One investigator[19] points out that "the screening and treatment methods [are] woefully inadequate as programs for the detection and treatment of serious emotional maladjustment." He suggested the reasons for this were the uncertainty of treatment and the fact that not all children who need treatment can receive treatment, the absence of good screening method, and lack of public acceptance of the emotionally disturbed child.

Until such time when the emotionally disturbed child can readily be identified as one in need of special educational opportunities, and all disciplines can join together in working toward better adjustment for these children, there can be little hope for widespread provisions. This is another area of special education in which much needs to be done.

Birch[20] finds current practices for the maladjusted child taking three directions: general prevention, correction in the classroom, and special classes and schools. He points out that in no situation are special classes and schools being established without general prevention and correction in the classroom also taking place. After writing to the fifty largest cities and obtaining information from them, he described their programs for maladjusted children. Among those he reported were:

Baltimore: A special day school is operated for boys 11–16 years of age who "present problems of school adjustment and whose needs cannot be met adequately in the regular grades."

Chicago: Social Adjustment Schools include three special schools and six adjustment centers (special classes in the regular elementary school). Two of the special schools are day schools for boys, with branches for

---

[19] Henry J. Dupont, "Emotional Maladjustment and Special Education," *Exceptional Children*, Vol. 24, No. 1 (September 1957), p. 14.

[20] Jack W. Birch, "Special Classes and Schools for Maladjusted Children," *Exceptional Children*, Vol. 22 (May 1956), pp. 332–37.

girls. The boys' schools operate on a twelve-month basis. The Chicago Home for Girls is a semiprivate residential institution for girls.

Cincinnati: Two classes for high school boys "with a high incidence of truancy" are operated within a regular high school as are two residential schools, one for boys and one for girls between the ages of 10 and 17. The County Welfare Department operates the two residential schools.

Dade County: Three social adjustment schools operated by the Board of Public Instruction in cooperation with the County Home and the Juvenile Court. The Juvenile Court places children in these schools on the basis of "delinquency or dependency."

Detroit: Three special schools for "problem boys" over 12 years of age operate in a wing of a regular elementary school, but under separate administration. Twelve special classes for "maladjusted" boys between the ages of 7 and 12 are operated within the regular elementary schools. A summer day camp program is also offered for these children.

Los Angeles: Two welfare classes for maladjusted boys and girls are offered in the elementary school, four more for boys only.

New York City: "The '600' School Program in New York City includes 14 schools for children with severe social and emotional disturbances." Five of these are day schools for boys 9–16, two are in residential settings for those awaiting court action, four are in children's institutions and three are in psychiatric hospitals.

Philadelphia: Two day and one residential schools are maintained for "children whose behavior does not permit an adjustment in the regular grades."

An alarming development in many communities is the grouping of dependent with delinquent children, somehow with the false notion that because the juvenile court is concerned with both types, they can best be provided for when grouped together. Or, perhaps, the thinking is that since the number may not be great enough to provide for each group separately, bringing them together for some schooling is better than none at all. Common sense alone should forbid such practices. The dependent child has all the characteristic background of the delinquent, and to place him with this type of child for any reason is an almost certain guarantee that he will develop along delinquent lines.

There are a number of instruments and rating sheets for screening emotionally disturbed children, but "few are or would be used by teachers and most are diagnostically, not screening, oriented."[21] Identifying those children in need of help is undoubtedly the greatest

21 Eli M. Bower, "The Emotionally Handicapped Child and the School," *Exceptional Children*, Vol. 26, No. 5 (January 1960), pp. 232.

problem facing the teacher. Numerous attempts are being made to provide teachers with guides, and patterns to follow, but the best guide will be more extensive training in child development. Through better understanding of children, the teacher will be in the position not only to identify emotional problems but also to provide early remedies for minor problems so that they do not become serious problems. She will also be in position to know when a problem is one that should be referred to a specialist.

Redl has worked with delinquent boys in residential treatment centers.

> He founded the Detroit Group Project in 1948, directed and conducted a "group therapy home" in Detroit called Pioneer House, and directed the child research branch of the National Institute of Mental Health. Redl's outstanding contribution has been made through his intensive study of the emotions of delinquent boys which has increased our understanding of the reason for hate, anger, and fear in these boys, and through his description of the process of treatment by ego development.[22]

Redl with Wattenburg stresses the relationship between mental health and education.[23]

The use of "nondirective" treatment for the emotionally disturbed child has been advocated by Rogers and Axline.[24,25] Rogers believes that the school environment is not an appropriate setting for therapy for emotionally disturbed children and suggests that the school work in conjunction with treatment agencies.[26] Axline allows permissiveness, but only to the extent that it provides for the child to express his feelings freely.[27] She stresses the relationship between teacher and child.

An experimental program described by Bower[28] included a listing of the types of administrative adjustments being tried.

[22] Norris G. Haring and E. Larkin Phillips, *Educating Emotionally Disturbed Children* (New York: McGraw-Hill Book Co., Inc., 1962), p. 25.

[23] Fritz Redl and William W. Wattenburg, *Mental Hygiene in Teaching* (New York: Harcourt, Brace & World, Inc., 1951).

[24] Carl R. Rogers, *Counseling and Psychotherapy* (Boston: Houghton Mifflin, 1951).

[25] Virginia Axline, *Play Therapy* (Boston: Houghton Mifflin, 1947).

[26] Norris G. Haring and E. Larkin Phillips, *Educating Emotionally Disturbed Children* (New York: McGraw-Hill Book Co., Inc., 1962), p. 48.

[27] Norris G. Haring and E. Larkin Phillips, *Educating Emotionally Disturbed Children* (New York: McGraw-Hill Book Co., Inc., 1962), p. 49.

[28] Bower, *loc. cit.,* pp. 237–38.

1. Adjustment Class (elementary): The grouping of handicapped children into one class of approximately 10–15 children with one teacher.

2. Adjustment Class (secondary): The grouping of emotionally handicapped adolescents for at least three full periods with core teacher and placement in selected electives.

3. Special Placement (elementary): A small, specially selected, regular class into which two or three emotionally handicapped children are placed.

4. Mental Health Consultation to Teachers (elementary and secondary): This entails no changes in class or program; teachers receive mental health consultation services on regular basis.

5. Child Study Program (elementary): This is the program of child study as outlined by the University of Maryland Institute of Child Study.

6. Social Living Class (secondary): A small group of adolescents who meet regularly with a guidance counselor or school psychologist. The program is generally informational and counseling centered.

7. Adolescent Group Counseling (secondary): A small group of adolescents who meet regularly with a clinical psychologist or social worker. The program is discussion centered, dealing in general with the emotional aspects of the student's problems.

8. Remedial Reading (elementary): The service of a remedial reading specialist is provided for small groups of retarded readers during regular class time or after school hours.

9. Play Activity (elementary): An after-school program of permissive play for young students. The "club" leader is a teacher.

10. Human Relations Classes (elementary and secondary): Human relations taught as part of the regular curriculum through stories, skits, and discussion.

11. Parent Group Counseling (elementary): Parents of children with emotional and learning problems meet with a group worker once a week.

12. Child Care—Home Economics Program (secondary): Emotionally handicapped girls are scheduled into a home economics program, care and observation of young children.

13. Identification Procedures (elementary): The process of screening as employed in all the other programs is carried out with no followup other than what the teacher takes responsibility for.

In an experiment carried out under the direction of Cruickshank,[29] two experimental and two control groups were placed in three public elementary schools. In all the groups there were both emotionally disturbed and brain-injured children. The results clearly indicated that the hyperactive, emotionally disturbed child was

---

[29] William Cruickshank, Frances A. Bentzen, Frederick H. Ratzeburg, and Marion T. Tannhauser, *op. cit.*

highly successful when measured by academic standards in the type of environment so highly recommended for the brain-injured child.

The juvenile delinquent is coming more and more to be a problem of special education. There seems to be some agreement that for the most part the juvenile delinquent can be educated in the regular class, although there is a small minority of delinquent children who will probably need special class or program assignment. In order for the delinquent to be educated in the regular classroom, however, the school must provide that type of situation which provides specialized services as well as suitable academic or vocational programs. The problem of the delinquent was stated well by Quay and Peterson:[30]

> Over the long-range period the only satisfactory approach to *treatment* of delinquency will be the *prevention* of delinquency through the understanding of the psychological and social causes of delinquent behavior and through the valid identification of the delinquent-prone.

The findings of the NEA Juvenile Delinquency Project[31] are reported in *Delinquent Behavior: Culture and the Individual* and *Delinquent Behavior: Principles and Practices*. The former publication is primarily theoretical; the latter provides information for public schools which they might utilize to solve some of the problems of juvenile delinquency.

Summary

The perceptually handicapped or brain-injured child discussed in this chapter is that type of child described by Strauss. Because the term "cerebral palsied" is such a misnomer for this child, although its use persists, "brain-injured" or "perceptually handicapped" seem to the author to better describe this child in terms of either cause or effect. But because so little is known about brain injury, and not all brain-injured children have the characteristics described by Strauss, much objection has arisen to the use of this

---

[30] Herbert Callister Quay and D. R. Peterson, "Personality Factors in the Study of Juvenile Delinquency," *Exceptional Children*, Vol. 26 (May 1960), p. 476.

[31] William C. Kvaraceus and Walter B. Miller, *Delinquent Behavior: Culture and the Individual;* and William C. Kvaraceus and William E. Ulrich, *Delinquent Behavior: Principles and Practices* (Washington, D.C.: NEA Juvenile Delinquency Project, 1959).

manner of identification. Fortunately, another perhaps better label has been suggested—the "Strauss syndrome" child.

One danger in drawing attention to the Strauss syndrome is that it superficially appears to fit almost every behavior and learning problem in a teacher's classroom. The diagnosis of this type of child is essentially a medical and psychological problem, although in some instances programs consisting of unlabeled children of suspected brain-damage have been established with only psychological evaluation. The ideal diagnostic program would include both psychiatric and psychological reports, along with case workers' reports and teachers' observations. There will be many cases which the medical examiner cannot diagnose definitively, but with supporting evidence from allied fields he should be able to make a tentative diagnosis.

The long-range results of special classes for the Strauss syndrome child cannot yet be evaluated. Only at the Cove Schools have specialized programs been underway long enough to give more than an immediate type of positive picture. The reports of the Cove Schools are most encouraging, however, and the preliminary reports of public school programs are also encouraging.

Socially and emotionally disturbed children are daily becoming a greater problem in American society. Urbanization and changing patterns of family responsibilities undoubtedly have been contributing factors to the increase of this problem. The public schools have begun to accept this problem as one within their realm of responsibility. The effectiveness of such programs depend to a large extent upon the degree of cooperation between psychiatric, psychological, and educational personnel.

CHAPTER VII

Looking Ahead

The author has attempted in this monograph to present an overview of the area of exceptional children. He has included in the area of "exceptionality" all children who differ from the average in such a way that they need special adjustments made within their environment. From an educator's point of view, of course, this difference in the needs of the child relates specifically either to the methods by which the child learns, the environment in which he learns, or the need for treatment or therapy of a type which will necessitate special scheduling of the child.

It is important to realize that the special class is not necessarily the place where the exceptional child is capable of learning best, nor is the special class the only concern of "special education." The current interest in homogeneous grouping has unfortunately led many to think that merely placing together children who seem to be somewhat alike is sound practice. At best, the establishment of a special class is only an administrative device. This, in itself, accomplishes little if any real gain for the exceptional child. Special classes for any type of exceptionality have value only if the children are placed in such a class with the positive understanding that their needs can better be met in such a situation, and if the teaching methods and materials are adjusted to meet the needs of this particular child.

It must be remembered that the large majority of schools in the United States are very small. To imply that special classes are the only concern of those in the area of special education for exceptional children would deny to children in small schools any hope of an adequate education. Fortunately, special education is concerned with the exceptional child in whatever situation he may be. Those who believe that special education and special classes are synonymous, have fortunately come to be in the minority.

Areas of Exceptionality

It has repeatedly been stated that the exceptional child is one who is different from the average. Traditionally, this difference was in intellectual areas, physical areas, or adjustment areas, but with increasing concern for other types of atypical children the term "exceptional child" is coming to include a much broader scope. Intellectual exceptionality deals with both those above and below average. The area of mental retardation has until recent years received the greatest amount of attention. Since Sputnik I, however, the other end of the intellectual range, the "gifted" child, has received increasingly more attention. Caution needs to be observed in over-enthusiasm for any particular type of exceptional child, and in particular against the crash program which only satisfies the needs of a small group in a temporary manner. The program for mentally retarded children has developed slowly but soundly, so that there is no negative feeling toward the added expense of such a program or question as to the value of such programs. The great rush to "do something for the gifted" endangers sound programs for the gifted as well as adjustments for individual gifted children. Careful planning, not merely to build a program for this school year, but to plan for a continuing program for gifted children in the future is urgently needed.

Exceptionality also deals with physical areas, but the area of physical exceptionality has been concerned primarily with the handicapped child. Perhaps incorrectly, the area of superior physical development has been relegated to the athletic departments, outside of the field of special education. By all possible criteria, however, the child with superior physical development should come under the area of the exceptional child. The exploitation of the athlete in years past is perhaps the best caution educators can hold before themselves when developing programs for the intellectually superior child.

In addition to cerebral palsy, the child with muscular coordination difficulties, the polio victim, and the child crippled by deformity or injury, exceptionality also concerns itself with health and all types of related problems.

The perceptually handicapped, Strauss syndrome, or brain-injured child is also a concern of those dealing with exceptional children. The newness of this area makes it one of the most controversial, but out of this controversy must come better understanding of this type of child and better educational provisions for him.

Social and emotional maladjustments are being viewed as problems involving exceptional children. The needs of these particular children, both educational and therapeutic, clearly justifies their being problems of those dealing with special education. Even such areas as juvenile delinquency are being recognized as proper to the area of special education.

The all-inclusive matter with which special education concerns itself has been criticized. The ultimate goal of providing better for all children, however, necessitates all-inclusiveness. Special education is not generally attempting to provide for children in any manner different from that of other educational programs, but if and when modifications are needed, special education does provide them. The ultimate goal is, of course, to aid each child in such a way that whenever possible he can be instructed in the regular classroom.

Changing Attitudes

It is not likely that any child is as much affected by the attitudes others have toward him as is the exceptional child. Primarily because the exceptional child is different from the stereotype of the "average" child, the attitudes of other children toward him symptomatize lack of understanding of individual differences. For this reason, it is vitally important that the exceptional child be accepted by his peer group. All those who work with exceptional children must constantly be aware of the importance of the attitudes of those with whom the child comes in contact. The attitude of the exceptional child toward himself is determined to a large extent by the attitudes of those around him.

A society such as ours, which has placed such great emphasis upon conformity, presents many problems for the exceptional child. He cannot be like other children, and knowing that all individuals are different to some degree does not mitigate for him his own problems.

Fortunately, the past decade has seen a great change in the attitude of the general public toward the exceptional child. Always easily moved by pity, the American public had for years supported areas of the physically handicapped, particularly those which were not so uncommon that the public had not had at least some direct contact with them, the diagnosis of which was clear of conflicting opinions. It is questionable that the attitude of the general public is one of acceptance, for pity does not necessarily imply understanding.

With increased attention to the exceptional child, however, a decided change has become evident. Instead of pitying the exceptional child, the general public has become interested in understanding such children. Initiating such movements have been groups of parents with exceptional children, but even these groups have frequently included other adults who are not so directly related to the problem. Volunteer workers willing to do more than just give money have become numerous. More information on all areas of exceptionality has been made available to the public. The attitude is not merely one of pity, but one of compassionately attempted understanding of the exceptional child. Out of this attempt has come acceptance. The public has come to realize that the exceptional child can usually profit from education adapted to his unique nature and needs.

Particularly noticeable has been the change in attitude toward the gifted child. The attitude of believing that such children cannot but make rapid progress because they are endowed with superior mental ability has changed to one of public obligation to provide adequately for the education of gifted children. The resulting change in the attitude of the gifted child is only now evolving. It will undoubtedly result in diminished attempt by the gifted child to conform to, but more understanding and acceptance on his part of, the average.

The most desirable attitude toward the exceptional child is one of acceptance and understanding. From such an attitude will logically flow the acceptance of responsibility for providing for such children in whatever manner is necessary to develop them to fullest potential. Never before has the climate for education been so favorable. Only to the extent that we continue to develop all children to the limit of their abilities will our democracy be strong.

The Changing Picture of the Exceptional Child

The entire area of exceptionality is rapidly advancing. Not only are new areas of exceptionality being identified, but existing areas are being expanded to include more of the children who could benefit by the special methods and procedures used to educate children with particular types of exceptionality. The definitions are becoming broader, but at the same time more specific. "Giftedness," for example, is no longer defined solely on the basis of intelligence test results. The area of the gifted also includes those children who show signs of potential leadership and creativity. As the area of the gifted is expanded to include those children who are potentially capable in any worthwhile line of endeavor, each of the sub-areas is being more carefully studied. Tests and procedures are being developed to identify children in each of these sub-areas.

More and more people, both the lay public and educators, are becoming aware of various areas of exceptionality. The characteristics of exceptional children are being widely disseminated so that where previously only a few people could be classified as "diagnosticians," today the general public as well as teachers alike are able to serve as scouts, utilizing informal but standardized screening devices, in order to refer possible exceptional children to the proper agencies. The need for early identification of all types of exceptionality is constantly stressed. Whether the child is above or below the norm in any area of exceptionality, early identification is essential for proper educational planning.

Trends

In 1962 President Kennedy appointed a panel of twenty-seven leaders in science, education, and other professions to develop a national coordinated program of research and services and to find new approaches to the solution of many basic problems in the field of mental retardation.

In "A Statement by the President Regarding the Need for a National Plan in Mental Retardation" the panel was commissioned to review and make recommendations with regard to personnel, major areas of concern, and means of encouraging research in determining the "relationships between the Federal Government, the States and private resources in their common efforts to eliminate mental retardation." With the concern of the President of the United States about the area of mental retardation, and the active commissioning of a planel to present plans, more and more national concern can be expected, not only in the area of mental retardation, but in all areas of exceptionality.

Undoubtedly the trend in the area of the exceptional child most outstanding is the increased amount of attention to all areas of exceptionality. More attention is being given at national, state, and local levels to the gifted, slow learner, physically handicapped, and emotionally disturbed than ever before.

Another trend is constant broadening of the concept of the exceptional. As the effectiveness of special education is demonstrated both through differentiated instruction within the regular classroom and in the special class situation, it is likely that other atypical children will also be considered exceptional. Such children as the culturally deprived, children from minority racial groups, children with particular learning problems, and perhaps many other types of exceptionality yet to be identified will be added to the ranks.

The sheltered workshop movement is making self-sufficient citizens out of individuals who are otherwise denied any of the advantages of a normal life by providing work experience for individuals who would otherwise be dependent upon relief for their livelihood. The rapid development of training programs in colleges throughout the country to train workers in the area of vocational rehabilitation is of utmost importance. Vocational rehabilitation has been primarily concerned with the rehabilitation of handicapped workers, but with the ever increasing industrialization and changes in types of needed employment, the responsibility for vocational retraining is being assumed by both federal and state governments. The emergence of state consultants in the area of the gifted is remarkable. Until only recently, there were no consultants at the state level in the area of the gifted. Today there are twelve. Those working at the state level have recently joined together as the Council of State Directors of Programs for the Gifted. The Southern Regional Education Board Project to train specialists in the area of the gifted to work at the state level is noteworthy. Under the direction of Ward at the University of Virginia, this Project accomplished effectively and in a short period gains for the gifted in an entire region.

Scope of Exceptional Children

It is generally stated that between ten and fifteen per cent of the school population come under the category of exceptional. It is not unlikely that this number will be much greater in the future, for a variety of reasons.

One of the major reasons for the expected increase in the number of exceptional children is the educational program concerning exceptionality that is being directed to the general public. As more and more people become aware of the various types of exceptionality, better and earlier identification will undoubtedly take place. Children who would have previously either been denied suitable opportunities because their area of exceptionality was unidentified or who would have been identified too late to benefit from existing provisions can now be identified early. This increased awareness on the part of the general public toward exceptionality can be expected to aid greatly the search for exceptional children at the pre-school level.

Although the discovery of such things as the Salk vaccine will reduce the number of polio victims, other crippling diseases are becoming more common. Research will continue to find cures and preventive measures, but it is not likely that progress will ever be made rapidly enough to reduce appreciably the total number of children with physical handicapping problems. One of the reasons for this is the success of medical research—children who would have previously not have lived are now able to lead relatively normal lives. These children are the concern of those in special education.

The problems and the rewards of working with exceptional children are not likely to diminish at any time in the near future. With increased research and knowledge of exceptional children, the role of special education will become increasingly important because the effectiveness of the effort will be increased. To some exceptional children this will mean return to the regular classroom situation, leaving the label "exceptional" behind. For others, it will mean adaptations in their behavioral and learning patterns, to fit as nearly as possible into their society. For still others, it will mean special adaptations to develop those gifts which they have, both for the betterment of society and individual self-realization.

Education

The role which education has played in the life of all children has changed radically. Of ever-increasing importance to him, consuming a larger portion of the child's time, education is more than just teaching the three R's. By law, every child between the ages of six and about sixteen must attend school. The upper limit has been gradually raised, and it is not unlikely that the lower limit will be lowered. Compulsory kindergartens are not yet a major part of the school systems, but they can be expected to become so in the future. Even a nursery school program may at some time in the future be an integral part of public schools.

The post-high school programs of adult education are of particular importance. Although they are directed only on a service basis for adults who wish to attend, they nevertheless are demonstrating the school's effectiveness as an "all life" agency.

The extension of the school program to earlier and later age levels is of particular significance to the exceptional child. Because it is so important that exceptionality be identified early, and since identification most often takes place when the child enters into group activities with other children of his own age, the nursery school-kindergarten program provides a means whereby the exceptional child can be identified earlier. The extension into adult programs provides a responsibility for those in special education to develop programs for exceptional individuals capable of benefiting by advanced or specialized training beyond the normal high school program.

The area of responsibility for trainable children is somewhat in dispute. Perhaps the strongest argument against the public schools assuming the responsibility for noneducable children, or those scoring below 50 IQ, is that they are an "all life" problem. Since the public school is no longer responsible beyond the ages of sixteen or seventeen, the argument is presented that these children should not be the responsibility of the public schools, but should be the responsibility of some agency dealing with children and adults. If the public school program is going to continue on beyond high school, in other than academic areas, then this argument is no longer legitimate when applied to the trainable child.

This is only one of the many problems which must be faced in dealing with exceptional children. Others are the methods by which exceptional children are taught, materials which are best suited to their needs, and the training of the people who are to work with exceptional children. Perhaps no final answers will ever be found to these problems, but it is readily apparent that partial answers already found make the effort worthwhile.

Problems

The area of exceptional children faces many problems. The greatest problem of all, that of the general public's attitude, has been faced realistically so that the exceptional child has to live no longer in fear of being different. This problem has not been completely overcome, but the attitude of the general public has so greatly changed that one has to believe it will continue to change.

Another problem yet to be solved deals with the constant drives for funds for each of many splinter groups concerned with exceptional children. The purpose of the Community Chest and United Fund drives was to consolidate appeals on the assumption that people would give more to one general appeal than they would to many small requests. An advantage of such general appeals was that groups requesting funds could be investigated and supervised so that the funds would not be misused. As these general appeal groups gain in strength and success, however, more and more splinter groups appear and make appeals for worthy causes, notably needy children. Many of these groups have been reluctant to join with the local community drive, because they would be unable to receive the same amount of support from the community had they been only one small part of a larger drive. So long as the number of these drives was limited, it presented no particular problem. Every year, however, has seen the addition of still more drives for aid to all areas of exceptionality, both those above and those below average ability or performance. The time is rapidly coming when all appeals will suffer because of the almost constant deluge of requests for funds for needy causes.

It is not likely that all such drives will join into one community group. It is not unlikely, however, that the overlapping groups will out of necessity join together into more effective appeals. There is no question but that the expenses of an exceptional child are much

greater than those of the average child, but whether the general
public will continue to support so many organizations and activities
is doubtful. The need for additional national organizations should
be questioned seriously, and where possible overlapping of goals and
areas of exceptionality should be avoided. A stronger, larger, more
inclusive organization would seem to be more advisable than a host
of splinter groups.

Another major problem in the area of the exceptional child is that
of recruiting personnel to work with these children. The general acceptance of the fact that exceptional children do have special needs
has been heartening. The willingness of states to support programs
for almost all areas of exceptionality is perhaps the best indication
of the change of attitude toward the exceptional child. But only if
personnel can be recruited and trained to work with these children
will the programs ever be developed. It is not good enough to take
into the area of exceptionality people who have been unsuccessful
with other groups of children. For the most part, only those successful with average children can be expected to be successful with
exceptional children.

Areas Needing More Attention

In the past ten years it has been popular to say that the gifted
child is the most neglected child in our school today. It is not unlikely that this has been true, and in terms of the potential good
which this child will do for society it is undoubtedly true and will
always be so. Fortunately, the gifted child can no longer be said to
be the most neglected, for he has at last come into his own right—
respected for his abilities, recognized as needing special educational
opportunities.

Those to whom the greatest amount of attention must be directed
now are the slow learner, emotionally and socially disturbed children, and perceptually handicapped children.

The needs of the slow learner, the child who is above the level of
those children being educated in special classes for mentally retarded, but still below that of the average, is very great. If for no
other reason than the large numbers of children in this category the
slow learner is the greatest problem we face today. To expect this
child to perform like the average is unrealistic and frustrating, both

for the teacher and the child. That this is the responsibility of the public schools has at last been accepted, and provisions for emotionally and socially disturbed children are gradually being developed within the public schools.

The need for identifying and providing for perceptually handicapped children is only in the beginning stages. The years ahead will undoubtedly see much progress in providing for them as for all other types of exceptional types of children.

Bibliography

GENERAL REFERENCE BOOKS ON EXCEPTIONAL CHILDREN

Abraham, Willard, *A Guide for the Study of Exceptional Children*. Boston. Porter Sargent, Publisher, 1955, 276 pp.

Baker, Henry J., *Introduction to Exceptional Children*, 3rd ed. New York: The Macmillan Company, 1959, 523 pp.

Cruickshank, William M., ed., *Psychology of Exceptional Children and Youth*. Englewood Cliffs, N.J: Prentice-Hall, Inc., 1955, 594 pp.

——— and G. Orville Johnson, eds., *Education of Exceptional Children and Youth*. Englewood Cliffs, N.J.: Prentice-Hall, Inc., 1958, 723 pp.

Frampton, Merle E. and Elena D. Gall, eds., *Resources for Special Education*. Boston: Porter Sargent Publisher, 1956, 250 pp. Gives listing of agencies, periodicals, books, pamphlets and articles for 22 specific areas of special education.

Garrison, Karl C. and Dewey G. Force, *Psychology of Exceptional Children*, 3rd ed. New York: The Ronald Press, 1959, 586 pp.

Goodenough, Florence L., *Exceptional Children*. New York: Appleton-Century-Crofts, 1956, 428 pp.

Heck, Arch O., *The Education of Exceptional Children*, 2nd ed. New York: McGraw-Hill Book Company, Inc., 1953, 513 pp.

Henry, Nelson B., ed., *The Education of Exceptional Children*, 49th Yearbook of the National Society for the Study of Education, Part II. Chicago: The University of Chicago Press, 1950, 356 pp.

Jordan, Thomas E., *The Exceptional Child*. Columbus, Ohio: Charles E. Merrill Books, Inc., 1962, 352 pp.

Kirk, Samuel A., *Educating Exceptional Children*. Boston: Houghton Mifflin Company, 1962, 415 pp.

Magary, James F. and John R. Eichorn, eds., *The Exceptional Child*. New York: Holt, Rinehart & Winston, Inc., 1960, 561 pp.

Magnifico, L. X., *Education for the Exceptional Child*. New York: Longmans, Green and Co., 1958, 371 pp.

Roucek, Joseph S., ed., *The Unusual Child*. New York: Philosophical Library, 1962, 293 pp.

REFERENCE BOOKS IN SPECIAL AREAS

Abraham, Willard, *Common Sense About Gifted Children*. New York: Harper & Row, Publishers, 1958, 268 pp.

Davis, Hallowell and S. Richard Silverman, eds., *Hearing and Deafness,* rev. ed. New York: Holt, Rinehart & Winston, Inc., 1960, 573 pp.

Fliegler, Louis A., ed., *Curriculum Planning for the Gifted.* Englewood Cliffs, N.J.: Prentice-Hall, Inc., 1961, 414 pp.

Freehill, Maurice F., *Gifted Children: Their Psychology and Education.* New York: The Macmillan Company, 1961, 412 pp.

Haring, Norris G. and E. Larkin Phillips, *Educating Emotionally Disturbed Children.* New York: McGraw-Hill Book Company, Inc., 1962, 322 pp.

Ingram, Christine P., *Education of the Slow-Learning Child,* 3rd ed. New York: The Ronald Press, 1960, 390 pp.

Kephart, Newell C., *The Slow Learner in the Classroom.* Columbus, Ohio: Charles E. Merrill Books, Inc., 1960, 292 pp.

Kirk, Samuel A. and G. Orville Johnson, *Educating the Retarded Child.* Cambridge, Mass.: The Riverside Press, 1951, 434 pp.

————, Merle B. Karnes, and Winifred D. Kirk, *You and Your Retarded Child.* New York: The Macmillan Company, 1956, 184 pp.

Lewis, Richard S., Alfred A. Strauss, and Laura E. Lehtinen, *The Other Child,* 2nd ed. New York: Grune and Stratton, 1960, 148 pp.

Lowenfeld, Berthold, *Our Blind Children: Growing and Learning With Them.* Springfield, Ill.: Charles C. Thomas, 1956, 205 pp.

Myklebust, Helmer R., *The Psychology of Deafness.* New York: Grune and Stratton, 1960, 393 pp.

Pearson, Gerald, *Emotional Disorders of Children.* New York: Norton and Co., 1949, 368 pp.

Perry, Natalie, *Teaching the Mentally Retarded Child.* New York: Columbia University Press, 1960, 185 pp.

Phillips, E. Lakin, Daniel N. Wiener, and Norris G. Haring, *Discipline, Achievement, and Mental Health.* Englewood Cliffs, N.J.: Prentice-Hall, Inc., 1960, 198 pp.

Riessman, Frank, *The Culturally Deprived Child.* New York: Harper & Row, Publishers, 1962, 140 pp.

Rosenzweig, Louis E. and Julia Long, *Understanding and Teaching the Dependent Retarded Child.* Darien, Conn.: The Educational Publishing Co., 1960, 185 pp.

Rothstein, Jerome H., *Mental Retardation.* New York: Holt, Rinehart & Winston, Inc., 1961, 628 pp.

Sarason, Seymour B. and Thomas Gladwin, *Psychological Problems in Mental Deficiency* (3rd ed.), ed. Gardner Murphy. New York: Harper & Row, Publishers, 1959, 678 pp.

Smith, H. Michal, ed., *Management of the Handicapped Child.* New York: Grune and Stratton, 1957, 276 pp.

Strauss, Alfred A. and Newell C. Kephart, *Psychopathology and Education of the Brain-Injured Child,* Volume II: *Progress in Theory and Clinic.* New York: Grune and Stratton, 1955, 266 pp.

Sumption, Merle R. and Evelyn M. Luecking, *Education of the Gifted.* New York: The Ronald Press, 1960, 499 pp.

Travis, Lee E., ed., *Handbook of Speech Pathology*. New York: Appleton-Century-Crofts, Inc., 1957, p. 1088.

Ward, Virgil S., *Educating the Gifted*. Columbus, Ohio: Charles E. Merrill Books, Inc., 1961, 240 pp.

Witty, Paul, ed., *The Gifted Child*. Boston: D. C. Heath and Co., 1951, 338 pp.

Index

Index

A

Above-average child, mentally (*see* Bright child; Gifted child; Intellectually superior; Very gifted child)
Academically talented, 30
The Academically Talented Secondary School Pupil, N.E.A. Invitational Conference on, 30
Accelerated programs for the gifted, 34-35
Advanced placement program for the gifted, 35
American Association for Gifted Children, 29, 31
American Association on Mental Deficiency, 12
American Foundation for the Blind, 48
American Medical Association, 46
American Printing House for the Blind, 48
Aphasia, expressive and receptive, 54
Arkansas, 24
Articulation problems, 54, 55
Athlete, 61, 68-69, 96
  exploitation of, 96

B

Baltimore, 88
Below-average child, mentally (*see* Educable mentally retarded; Intellectually handicapped; Severely mentally retarded (trainable); Slow learner)
Binet-Simon scales, 28
and Stanford Revision, 28, 38
Blindness, the blind and the partially seeing, 44-48, 72-73
  causes, 46
  education of, 47-48
  incidence, 44, 47
  partially seeing, 47
  screening tests, 45-46
Blue babies, 67
Braille, 48
Brain-injured (*see* Perceptually handicapped; Strauss syndrome)

B (cont.)

Bright child, 30-31
  academically talented, 30
  curricular adjustments for, 30-31
  defined, 30
  enrichment classes for, 30
  I.Q. range, 30
The Bronx School of Science, New York City, 36

C

CNS impairment, 78
Cardiac conditions, 64-67
Cerebral palsy and the cerebral palsied, 55, 62-64, 78, 82
  associated with mental, speech, and hearing problems, 64
  causes, 64
  census, 64
  educational provisions for, 64
Chicago, 88-89
Chicago Home· for Girls, 89
Classroom teacher:
  and speech handicapped, 57-58
  in testing program, 10-11
Cleveland, 28, 30, 35
The Colfax Plan for gifted children, 35
Council of State Directors of Programs for the Gifted, 100
The Cove Schools for the perceptually handicapped, 83, 93
Creativity and intelligence, 33-34, 70
Crippled (*see* Orthopedically handicapped)

D

Dade County, Fla., 89
Day care centers for the severely mentally retarded, trainable, 23-24 ·
Deafness, the deaf and the hard of hearing, 49-53, 73
  causes, 49-50
  education of, 51-52
  personal adjustment, 50-51
  prevalence, 49
  and speech, 50-51
Decibel, 50-54
Delicate child, 64-65

113

INDEX

Special classes, 5
  bases for assignments to, 10-11
  for the blind and partially seeing, 47-48
  for the bright child, 30
  for the deaf, 51
  for the disturbed child, 88-89
  for the educable mentally retarded, 18, 20
  for the gifted child, 28, 30, 34-37
  for the health-problem children, 65
  for the juvenile delinquent, 92
  for the orthopedically handicapped, 63
  for the perceptually retarded, 84, 93
Special education, 4-6, 95-96
  administrative procedures in, 5
  beneficial to the regular educational program, 5-6
  defined, 5
  a democratic procedure, 4
  harmful appeals for, to the public, 6
  not limited to special classes, 5, 95
  statistics on its growth, 5
Special schools:
  for the deaf, 51
  for the disturbed child, 88-89
  for the educable mentally retarded, 18
  for the gifted child, 36
  for the health-problem children, 65
  for the orthopedically handicapped, 63
Speech development, normal and retarded, 55
Speech problems (*see also* Stuttering), 53-58, 73
  classifications, 54-56
  educational provision for, 57-58
  prevalence, 53
  speech therapy, 58
  terminology, 54

Speech reading, 54
Strauss syndrome (*see also* Perceptually handicapped), 71, 78-85, 92-93
Stuttering, 54, 56-57
  sex ratio, 56

T

Teacher training for work with the mentally retarded, 21-22
Telebinocular, 45, 46
Totally dependent child (*see also* Dependent child), 12
Tuberculosis, 62, 63, 64
Two-track vs. single-track plan for educating the mentally retarded, 19

U

Underachiever among the gifted, 32-33
U.S. Children's Bureau, 45
U.S. Office of Naval Research, 45

V

Very gifted child (*see also* Gifted child), 38-41
  I.Q. range, 38
  studies of adjustment and achievement, 38-41
Virginia, University of, 100
Visual acuity, 45-46
Vocational rehabilitation and retraining programs, 100

W

Washington University, School of Medicine, 45
West Virginia, 24